Didn't the Gospel work?

- At 16, Keith Phillips directed the Los Angeles Youth for Christ clubs.
- At 21, he led 300 college volunteers in teaching weekly Bible clubs.
- At 24, as president of World Impact, he could count thousands of decisions for Christ.
- At 25, he almost quit!

Those who had come to accept Christ through his ghetto ministry were living lives that were the same or worse than before. When Keith Phillips came to grips with the importance of discipleship, his ministry was revolutionized. In *The Making of a Disciple,* he displays Jesus' standard for maturity and demonstrates how you can achieve this standard and reproduce it in the lives of others.

The Making of a Disciple

KEITH PHILLIPS

SPIRE BOOKS

Fleming H. Revell Company
Old Tappan, New Jersey

Scripture quotations not otherwise identified are from the New American Standard Bible, Copyright © THE LOCKMAN FOUNDATION 1960, 1962, 1963, 1968, 1971, 1972, 1973, 1975 and are used by permission.

Scripture quotations identified KJV are from the King James Version of the Bible.

Scripture quotations identified LB are from The Living Bible, Copyright © 1971 by Tyndale House Publishers, Wheaton, Illinois 60187. All rights reserved.

Scripture quotations identified NIV are from HOLY BIBLE New International Version, copyright ©, New York International Bible Society, 1978. Used by permission.

Scripture quotations identified RSV are from the Revised Standard Version of the Bible, copyrighted 1946, 1952, © 1971 and 1973.

Some of the names in this book have been changed to protect the privacy of the individual.

Library of Congress Cataloging in Publication Data
Phillips, Keith W
    The making of a disciple.
       1. Christian life—1960–   I. Title.
BV4501.2.P527   248.4   80-24908
ISBN 0-8007-8485-5

TO Patrick Delaney, Susie Krehbiel, Fred Stoesz, Mary Thiessen and Thuan Vuong, fellow disciple-makers, whose commitment to bringing God's love to the ghettos of America is a constant source of encouragement.

CONTENTS

Introduction

Jesus came to save a fallen race and raise up a people who would praise Him forever. In the discharge of this mission, He ministered among us as a servant, caring for the sick, healing the brokenhearted, and preaching the Gospel to the multitudes. But through it all He concentrated His attention upon the making of disciples—persons who would learn of Him and follow in His steps.

After His death and resurrection, before ascending back to heaven, He told these followers to "go and make disciples of all nations." They could understand what He meant, for He was only asking them to continue what He had practiced with them. The Great Commission is not a summons to a new course of action, but the explication of His own way of mission.

Ingenious in its simplicity, this was the essence of Christ's plan to reach the world for God. He knew that it could not fail. For true disciples will not only grow in the likeness of their Master; in time, by His Spirit, they will reproduce His life in others.

What is also apparent, this strategy brings the thrust of Jesus' ministry within the vocation of every Christian. To be sure, not many are called to pastor a great congregation or even teach a Sunday School class, but everyone is called to participate in the making of disciples. His commission is not a special gift; it is a command, and all who believe on Christ have no option but to obey.

Yet this obligation is scarcely perceived in the church

7

today. Not that the mandate is denied, but that most people have no idea how it relates to the daily work of their lives.

That is why this book is so welcome. It gets down to the practical aspects of discipling. Writing out of wide experience in this ministry, Dr. Keith Phillips shares principles he has learned in the plodding, painstaking process of leading persons in the way of Christ.

He builds on the premise that developing character is more important than polishing skills. "You must be God's person," he writes, "before you can do God's work." Basic to this approach is the Biblical necessity of one dying to self-centeredness, so that Christ has undisputed rule in the heart. Undergirding this commitment is an attitude of submissiveness to divine authority, a devotion reflected in strong personal discipline, outgoing love, and a sense of community.

The author goes on to detail how such growth is fostered, pointing out essential ingredients in the life of both the discipler and the discipled. You will see that it is not an easy task. And there are no short cuts. To do this work one must have resolute determination and sacrificial compassion.

Here is where, finally, all of us must face the issue. Are we willing to pay the price? Trusting that this book will help us realize more the need, and inspire us toward a confident, purposeful involvement in our Master's work, it is a pleasure to commend it to you.

Robert E. Coleman

SECTION I

What Is Discipleship?

1
Make Disciples, Not Converts

The first month I was in Watts I witnessed a murder.

Ronnie was a spunky little kid bursting with energy. He attended the children's Bible club I had begun a few weeks earlier in a federal housing project. He caught my attention on this particular day because he was walking barefoot across a field covered with broken glass. I could not imagine how he kept his feet from being slashed to pieces. Yet he didn't seem to have a care in the world.

Suddenly an older boy dashed up to Ronnie, stabbed him in the chest, grabbed his transistor radio and ran. Ronnie dropped to the ground.

I couldn't believe it. I broke into a cold sweat. My palms turned clammy. My heart raced as I ran toward him. I was afraid someone would ask me to help. I wanted to, but I didn't know what to do. So I stood lost in the crowd.

The reaction of the children and teenagers who had gathered around Ronnie's body stunned me. I expected hostility and outrage, but instead they acted as if they were at a carnival. They booed when the police came and cheered when the ambulance arrived. They laughed, hollered and tried to outdo each other with stories about other killings they had seen. No one seemed to care about Ronnie. Even his own brother showed no grief.

I stood there for what seemed like an eternity. What was

utterly horrifying to me had apparently been just a common event for everyone else. But this was only the beginning, the first in a series of shocks that were to break my heart for this mission field to which God had called me.

As I walked away from the field where Ronnie died, a youngster named Jimmy matter-of-factly told me, "It ain't no big thing. People get killed around here all the time. My one-year-old cousin was killed a couple months ago. He was screaming at two in the morning 'cause he was sick. His mother was real mad. She grabbed him out of bed and threw him out the window. His head broke . . . ."

The more I listened, the more I learned.

Not one of the children I met knew his father. It didn't seem to bother them. That's just the way it was.

At first I could not believe Darrell was telling me the truth when he said he had not eaten for three days. I knew that no one went hungry in America. I thought he was trying to con me. But then I found out that his mother, an addict, spent their meager income on narcotics.

I knew twelve-year-old Teresa had a child, but was puzzled when she told me that her baby was her brother. Later I discovered it was Teresa's father who had gotten her pregnant.

There was sixteen-year-old Rhonda, a mother of two weeks, who could not put up with her baby's crying. She got high on drugs and beat her son with her fists, breaking his ribs and puncturing his lungs.

Nine-year-old Belinda lived in constant terror of sexual abuse from her uncle. Her mother did not care. Her brothers and sisters just laughed and made fun of her.

The horrendous deterioration and despair in the ghetto staggered me. It was like stepping into a different world: hunger, abuse, drugs, death, twelve-year-old mothers, illegitimate children. Nobody batted an eye. Nobody cared.

I knew that Jesus must be the answer to these great physical and spiritual needs. But I had no idea how to make the gospel relevant to the ghetto.

The only approach that occurred to me was mass evangelism. So I started children's Bible clubs in Watts. Scores of kids came. They all wanted to "accept Jesus"! And they all wanted to bring their friends. Mothers appreciated their kids "getting religion," and teenagers were anxious to know when clubs would begin for them. Within a few years 300 Christian college volunteers joined me in teaching weekly Bible studies to hundreds of children.

We organized evangelistic meetings. Many people attended—some just to see "those white folks." I would preach a simple salvation message, and invariably almost everyone would raise his hand to indicate a desire to have his sins forgiven and to be at peace with God. Meticulously we filled out decision cards and faithfully sent follow-up material to each new convert, not realizing that many of them were illiterate.

I would pray with an addict or a neglected child, say "God bless you," and then leave. Since I could not possibly shepherd all these new Christians, I reasoned that the Holy Spirit would take care of them.

Hundreds of people in the Los Angeles ghetto "accepted Christ." My friends patted me on the back and assured me that I was doing a fine job. I wanted to believe them. And for a while, I did.

But as the months blended into years, I had to admit that there was a serious problem. With all of these decisions for Christ there should have been changed lives—hundreds of them. But as hard as I looked, I could not find even one! Something had gone wrong.

Partly because of pride, partly because of ignorance, I kept hoping things would somehow right themselves. But I could not shake the gnawing feeling that everything had been in vain. There was no lasting fruit. The turnover rate in my Bible clubs was too great. Different youngsters came every week. Teenagers who had learned of Christ as children were still friendly, but they had become pimps, prostitutes or pushers. Former Bible club kids were running with street gangs. It seemed as if the gospel had not worked.

I was discouraged. I almost quit.

In desperation I went to God's Word. For the first time in my life I wanted to see what *God* said, rather than to prove what I already knew.

As I read Matthew 28:19,20, I received a startling revelation. Christ's commission to His Church was not to "make converts," but to "make disciples." That was it! Even though I did not understand all the implications, I knew immediately that discipleship had been the missing ingredient in my ministry.

I had hundreds of notches on my evangelistic belt, but I could not locate one maturing Christian. I had proclaimed the gospel, but I had failed to make disciples.

The more I studied the New Testament, the firmer my new conviction became. Discipleship is the only way to avoid malnourishment and weakness in the spiritual children for whom I am responsible. It is the only method which will produce mature Christians who can reverse the physical and spiritual decay in the ghetto.

I knew God was grieved by my initial approach to the ministry. I made a commitment that from that point on I would focus every resource the Lord would give me on making disciples.

2
What Is Discipleship?

During the Golden Age of Greece the young Plato could be seen strolling through the streets of Athens in pursuit of his master: the shabby, barefoot and brilliant Socrates. Here, probably, was the beginning of discipleship. Socrates wrote no books. His students listened intently to every word he spoke and watched everything he did in preparation to teach others. Apparently the system worked; Plato later founded the Academy, where philosophy and science continued to be taught for 900 years.

Jesus used a similar relationship with the men He trained in order to spread the kingdom of God. His disciples were with Him day and night for three years. They listened to His sermons and memorized His teachings. They saw Him live the life He taught. Then, after His ascension, the disciples entrusted the words of Christ to others and encouraged them to adopt His life-style and obey His teaching. A disciple is a student who memorizes the words, actions and life-style of his teacher in preparation to teach others.

Christian discipleship is a teacher-student relationship, based on the model of Christ and His disciples, in which the teacher reproduces the fullness of life he has in Christ in the student so well, that the student is able to train others to teach others.

A careful study of Christ's teaching and life reveals that discipleship has two essential components: self-death and reproduction. They keynote the entire ministry of Jesus. He died so that He could reproduce new life. And He requires each of His disciples to follow His example.

Self-Death

Christ's call to discipleship is a call to *self-death*, an absolute surrender to God. Jesus said, ". . . If anyone wishes to come after Me, let him deny himself, and take up his cross daily, and follow Me. For whoever wishes to save his life shall lose it, but whoever loses his life for My sake, he is the one who will save it" (Luke 9:23,24).

From the world's perspective, Christ's frankness in calling people to follow Him appears to be extreme. Today if a person wanted to "sell" such a demanding life-style, an all-consuming commitment, he would probably retain the most sophisticated Madison Avenue firm to meticulously describe the glorious benefits of such a decision in a full-color brochure. Or he would hire the most glamorous actress and surround her with "beautiful people" obviously enjoying the contentment and delight of their new life in Christ. Then he would catch the magic of the moment on videotape, which hopefully would be aired at halftime during "Monday Night Football."

But Jesus is honest and direct: to share in His glory a person must first share in His death.

Jesus is Lord of lords and King of kings. And the Lord of the universe commands every person to follow Him. His call to Peter and Andrew (Matthew 4:18,19) and to James and John (Matthew 4:21) was a command. "Follow Me" has always been a command, never an invitation (John 1:43).

Jesus never pleaded for someone to follow Him. He was embarrassingly straightforward. He confronted the woman at the well with her adultery, Nicodemus with his intellectual pride and the Pharisees with their self-righteousness.

No one can interpret "... Repent, for the kingdom of heaven is at hand" as begging (Matthew 4:17). Jesus commanded each person to renounce self-seeking pursuits, abandon his sin and obey Him completely.

When the rich young ruler refused to sell all and follow Him (Matthew 19:21), Jesus did not run after him trying to negotiate a compromise. He never watered down His standard. Jesus simply said, "Whoever serves me must follow me ..." (John 12:26 NIV).

Jesus expected immediate obedience. He accepted no excuses (Luke 9:62). When a man first wanted to bury his father before following Christ, He told him, "Follow me; and let the dead bury their dead" (Matthew 8:22 KJV). No man was praised for obeying Christ's command to follow Him and be His disciple; it was expected. Jesus said, "So you too, when you do all the things which are commanded you, say, 'We are unworthy slaves; we have done only that which we ought to have done'" (Luke 17:10).

So when do you become a Christian, a disciple of Christ? When you walk down an aisle? When you kneel at an altar? When you weep sincerely? Not necessarily. Christ's original followers became disciples when they obeyed Him, when they "immediately left the boat and their father, and followed Him" (Matthew 4:22).[1]

Obeying Christ's command, "Follow Me," results in self-death. Christianity without self-death is only an abstract philosophy. It is Christianity without Christ.

Perhaps the most fundamental error many Christians make is to separate receiving salvation and being a disciple.

---

[1] Our salvation is caused by and grounded in the grace of God. God's grace is the *source.* Our faith is the *instrument.* But our obedience is both the mandatory human *response* and the undeniable *evidence* of salvation (Ephesians 2:8–10). It is the proof of our faith. That is why James says "faith without works is dead" (James 2:17).

They place them on different levels of Christian maturity, assuming that it is acceptable to be saved without having to commit oneself to those more radical demands of Jesus, like "taking up the cross" and following Him (Matthew 10:38).

This assumption is grounded on the erroneous belief that salvation is primarily for man's benefit—to make him happy and to prevent eternal damnation.

While God's gift of salvation does meet man's most crucial need, this humanistic, do-it-for-your-own-good pitch completely ignores the ultimate reason Christ died on the cross. God provides man with salvation primarily to bring glory to Himself through people who have the character of His Son (Ephesians 1:12). God's glory is more important than man's welfare (Isaiah 43:7).

No one who understands the purpose of salvation would dare to speculate that a person might be saved without accepting Christ's Lordship. Christ cannot be the Lord of my life if I am the lord of my life. In order for Christ to be in control, I have to die. I cannot become a disciple without dying to myself and identifying with Christ who died for my sins (Mark 8:34). A disciple follows his Master, even to the cross.

For a long time I struggled to understand the practical implications of "self-death." How would this determined self-renunciation flesh itself out in my life? It finally registered while I was meditating on Galatians 2:20: "I have been crucified with Christ; and it is no longer I who live, but Christ lives in me. . . ."

Let's suppose that on January 1, I was flying over Kansas when the plane exploded. My body fell to the ground and I was dead on impact. Before long a farmer discovered my corpse. There was no pulse, no heartbeat, no breath. My body was cold. Obviously, I was dead. So the farmer dug a grave. But by the time he placed my body in the earth, it was too dark to cover it. Deciding he would finish in the morning, he returned home.

Then Christ came to me and said, "Keith, you are dead. Your life on earth is over. But I will breathe into you a breath of new life if you promise to do anything I ask and go anywhere I send you."

My immediate reaction was, "No way! That's unreasonable. It's slavery." But then I realized I was not in a good bargaining position, and I quickly came to my senses. I wholeheartedly agreed.

Instantly, my lungs, heart and other vital organs began to function again. I came back to life. I was born again! From that point on no matter what Christ asked me to do or where He asked me to go, I was more than willing. No task was too difficult, no hours too long, no place too dangerous. Nothing was unreasonable. Why? Because I had no claim to my life. I was living on borrowed time, Christ's time. Keith died on January 1 in a Kansas cornfield. Then I could say with Paul, "I have been crucified [have died] with Christ; and it is no longer [Keith] who is alive, but Christ [who] lives in me. . . ."

That is what self-death and being born again are all about. Christ's command to "Follow Me" is an injunction to participate in His death in order to experience new life. You become a living dead man, totally committed to Him.

A great paradox of life is that there is tremendous freedom in this death. A dead man is no longer concerned with his own rights, his independence or the opinions of others. When he was joined in a spiritual union with the crucified Christ, those things so highly prized by the world—riches, security and status—were relinquished. "Now those who belong to Christ Jesus have crucified the flesh with its passions and desires" (Galatians 5:24). A man who takes up the cross, one crucified with Christ, is not anxious about tomorrow because his future is in the hands of another.

One inner-city worker dreamed of establishing a daring street ministry. But when the miracles he had hoped for did not materialize, he resorted to fantasy, distorting encounters and creating imaginary events, hoping to stimulate the respect of others. He became enslaved to his visions of grandeur, a captive of his own expectations.

His subconscious motivation was to win the awe and admiration of the Christian world by performing heroic feats for the kingdom. His passions, dreams and visions were never crucified. He was never freed from the pressure to succeed and to produce. He never experienced that release which comes from having nothing to prove, nothing to lose. He had a perverted perception of discipleship. He wanted to serve God so that *he* could receive glory.

In contrast, a dead man is liberated to do all things to the glory of God (Romans 8:10). He places all that he is and everything that he has at God's permanent disposal. His submission to Christ's Lordship empowers him to please God in every decision he makes, every word he speaks and every thought he thinks. A disciple views his whole life and ministry as worship (1 Corinthians 10:31). Self-death frees him to enjoy his love affair with God.

Self-death is the mandatory precursor to becoming a disciple. Any person who has not experienced self-death cannot qualify as a legitimate link in the discipling process because he cannot reproduce. Jesus taught, ". . . unless a grain of wheat falls into the earth and dies, it remains by itself alone; but if it dies, it bears much fruit" (John 12:24). Without reproduction there is no discipleship.

Reproduction

Christ commanded His disciples to reproduce in others the fullness of life they found in Him (John 15:8). He warned that, "Every branch in Me that does not bear fruit, [My Father] takes away; and every branch that bears fruit, He prunes it, that it may bear more fruit" (John 15:2).

A mature disciple must teach other believers how to live a life pleasing to God and must equip them to train others to teach others. No person is an end in himself. Every disciple is part of a process, part of God's chosen method for expanding His kingdom through reproduction. We know this because Christ discipled men and commanded His disciples to make disciples (Matthew 28:19).

God could have selected any method He wanted to spread the gospel and build His kingdom. It was no accident that Greek was the world's common language long after that empire's demise. The Greek language has certain nuances that make it ideal for communicating truth. Also, the imperial Roman highways that united the known world may have been intended to carry her chariots, but the Christian gospel was their most valuable commerce.

Just as God used Greece and Rome as unwitting instruments to spread the gospel, He could have caused the printing press, radio or even television to be invented before Christ's birth. Jesus could have been a renowned author, a radio Bible teacher or the first TV evangelist. God's options were not limited.

But instead of adopting any of these sophisticated methods, Jesus opted for discipleship. He personally trained a small band of men and equipped them to train others to teach others. He commanded them to make disciples.

I must confess that at first I questioned Christ's wisdom. On the surface this investment in individuals appeared to be too slow. It took Jesus three years to disciple twelve men, and one of them failed.

I thought I would be fortunate if in three years I could train one person so well that he could join me in training others and at that rate I would never be able to make a dent in the 2 million people in the Los Angeles ghetto. At best I could only expect to disciple sixteen people in my lifetime. And what good would that do? My sin was that I doubted the wisdom and sovereignty of God.

But when I studied discipleship, I discovered God had chosen a solid and effective way to build His kingdom. It would start small, like a mustard seed, but grow rapidly as it spread from person to person throughout the world. His Church would be a dynamic movement, rather than a static structure. Discipleship is the only way to produce both the quantity and quality of believers God desires.

The Mathematics Are Sound

Can you imagine reaching over 4 billion people with the gospel? This task of fulfilling the Great Commission seems so staggering that even visionaries might be overwhelmed and wind up doing nothing. But the Bible is a method book as well as a message book. And Christ's method is to make disciples.

When I came to the ghetto, I had a passion for evangelism. Suppose that on the first day I led one person to Christ. Subsequently, I led another individual to Christ every day for the rest of the year. By the end of the year I would have directed 365 people to the Lord. If I continued to do that for the next thirty-two years, I would have reached 11,680. Quite an accomplishment!

On the other hand, suppose that I reached only one person for Christ that first year. This time, however, I discipled him for an entire year, so that he was thoroughly grounded in the Christian faith and became capable of reaching and discipling another. The next year the two of us each reached one additional person and trained those two to join us in training others. If we continued this for thirty-two years, there would be 4,294,967,296 disciples—the population of the world! (*See* table 1.)

TABLE 1
A Comparison of Discipleship and Evangelism

Year	Evangelist	Discipler
1	365	2
2	730	4
3	1095	8
4	1460	16
5	1825	32
6	2190	64
7	2555	128
8	2920	256
9	3285	512
10	3650	1024
11	4015	2048
12	4380	4096
13	4745	8192
14	5110	16,384
15	5475	32,768
16	5840	65,536
17	6205	131,072
18	6570	262,144
19	6935	524,288
20	7300	1,048,576
21	7665	2,097,152
22	8030	4,194,304
23	8395	8,388,608
24	8760	16,777,216
25	9125	33,554,432
26	9490	67,108,864
27	9855	134,217,728
28	10,220	268,435,456
29	10,585	536,870,912
30	10,950	1,073,741,824
31	11,315	2,147,483,648
32	11,680	4,294,967,296

Note: Assumes evangelist reaches one person a day, and discipler trains one person a year.

I mentioned my original hesitancy. But let me share my excitement now. If each of our present staff members in Los Angeles discipled one person every two years so well that their disciples could join us in training others, we could reach the entire Los Angeles ghetto—two million people— in thirty-two years. That means that I only have to invest in sixteen people in thirty-two years. And that is a manageable task.

Even though discipleship starts off slowly, in the long run spiritual multiplication reaches far more people in the same amount of time than addition. (*See* table 2.)

The Great Commission is feasible!

Quality Reproduction Is Ensured

If I were only involved in evangelism and responsible for over 11,000 new Christians, it would take me from September to December each year just to address a Christmas card to each of them. I would be so busy leading people to Christ that it would be impossible to care for them and help them grow. I would need a computer merely to recall their names. Such irresponsible evangelism would cause spiritual child neglect, and result in weak, superficial believers.

I used to brag about my evangelistic prowess—how I met a man on an airplane, talked with him for fifty minutes, led him to Christ, yet never knew his last name. Somehow, I believed exploits like that heightened my spiritual virility— until I realized I had deserted most of these "victims" after our brief encounters. I had experienced the excitement of conception and the joy of birth without assuming the responsibility of parenthood.

Let me illustrate the gravity of this failure.

In June of 1976, my wife, Katie, and I were blessed by the birth of twin boys, Joshua and Paul. Believe me, they demanded round-the-clock attention. We fed them, rocked

TABLE 2
A COMPARISON OF DISCIPLESHIP AND EVANGELISM

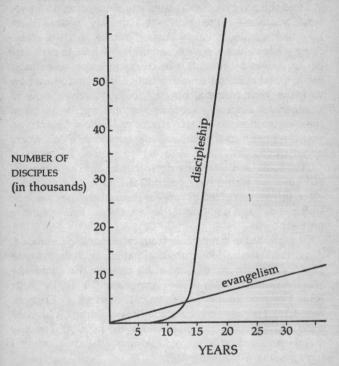

Note: Assumes evangelist reaches one person a day, and discipler trains one person a year.

them, changed their diapers and did everything good parents do.

Suppose that when the boys were three months old, Katie and I decided we needed a break (which we did). So we propped Joshua and Paul up against the couch to talk with them.

I told them we were exhausted and were going on a two-week vacation—alone. However I quickly assured them they had nothing to worry about. "You've watched everything we have done, so you should know how to take care of yourselves by now. But in case you forget something, we've typed out detailed instructions for you to follow: how to make your formula, how to feed yourselves, how to change your diapers, what the symptoms are. We've taped these instructions to the refrigerator and left our itinerary so you can phone us if you have any questions. Don't worry about a thing."

Had Katie and I actually done that to our three-month-old boys, we would have been thrown in jail for child neglect. Infants can't feed or care for themselves; they must be watched day and night until they are old enough to survive on their own.

Discipleship is inseparable from responsible parenthood. A spiritual parent, like a physical parent, is accountable to God for the care and nurture of his children. Paul knew he was the spiritual father of the Corinthians: ". . . for in Christ Jesus I became your father through the gospel" (1 Corinthians 4:15). He called the Galatians "my children" (Galatians 4:19) and Timothy "my true child in the faith" (1 Timothy 1:2). He pleaded on behalf of Onesimus, "my child, whom I have begotten" (Philemon 10).

The disciple-maker knows that his responsibility continues until his disciple becomes a spiritually mature, reproducing believer. He invests a great amount of time in his disciple and gives undivided attention to his needs. Discipleship is quality reproduction that ensures that the process of spiritual multiplication will continue from generation to generation.

God's Spirit instituted a safeguard to monitor the quality

of spiritual offspring. Paul indicates that the disciple-maker's relationship with his disciple extends through *four generations.* "And the things which you have heard from me in the presence of many witnesses, these entrust to faithful men, who will be able to teach others also" (2 Timothy 2:2). Here, Paul (first generation) instructs his spiritual son, Timothy (second generation), to teach the things that Paul taught him to faithful men (third generation), who in turn would teach others (fourth generation).

Paul's reference to four generations is no coincidence. A disciple-maker only knows how effectively he has taught his student when he sees his disciple's student teaching others.

In 1972 God called Al Ewert to direct our work in the Wichita ghetto. I discipled him. I spent hours and hours with Al over many months, instilling in him everything I knew about being God's man. We searched for biblical principles together and applied them to our lives. Before long Al began to disciple Don, who has since discipled Maurice.

In light of discipleship's mandate to train others to teach others, I (first generation) can only evaluate my effectiveness with Al (second generation) by watching how Don (third generation) is doing with Maurice (fourth generation). If Al fully grasps discipleship (self-death and reproduction), then Don will be well equipped to train Maurice how to train others to teach others. Maurice is the real proof of the pudding.

Four Generations

GENERATION	1	2	3	4
	Paul →	Timothy →	Faithful Men →	Others
	Keith →	Al ⟶	Don ⟶	Maurice

It is a human tendency to opt for mass production rather than quality workmanship. How often have you heard, "They just don't make things like they used to"? And how frequent the reply, "It's just not cost-effective"?

Only a master craftsman demands quality above all else. His reputation is at stake with every item produced because he places his name on his work. Jesus is the master disciple-maker. Since every believer bears His name, there is no room in discipleship for mediocrity.

Two thousand years ago Jesus addressed a great multitude of followers with uncompromising candor. He declared, "Whoever does not carry his own cross and come after Me cannot be My disciple" (Luke 14:27). Jesus narrowed every listener's options to two. If man's response is unbelief, he disobeys and dies. He is Christ's enemy (*see* Matthew 12:30). If he responds in faith, he obeys and becomes a disciple, dies to himself and reproduces. Christ is the Lord of his life. Jesus speaks of no other alternative.

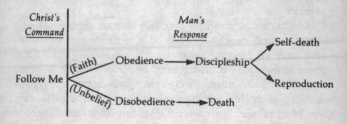

Christ knew that this would be the most momentous decision any person could make, so He warned them to count the cost (Luke 14:28). And as incomprehensible as it seems, many withdrew ". . . and walked no more with him" (John 6:66 KJV).

Christ's life-changing command, "Follow Me," is as all-encompassing today as it was on the Galilean coast. It cannot be taken lightly. Your eternal destiny hinges on your response.

You either retain your rights, possessions and your life as it is now, or you give up everything you have to the Lordship of Christ in exchange for eternal life and peace with God. Nothing would please Christ more than if, like Levi, you ". . . left everything, sprang up and went with him" (Luke 5:28 LB).

Christ's call still echoes through the centuries: "COME DIE WITH ME!"

Disciple's Checklist—*What Is Discipleship?*
☐ I have died to myself.
☐ I am reproducing in others the fullness of life I have in Christ.

SECTION II

Who Is a Disciple?

3

How Do You Know
If You Are a Disciple?

Many people claim to have experienced self-death and to be totally committed to Christ. But Jesus said, "Not everyone who says to Me, 'Lord, Lord,' will enter the kingdom of heaven; but he who *does* the will of My Father who is in heaven" (Matthew 7:21, *italics added*).

The experience of Ed, a friend of mine, illustrates the seriousness of mistaken identity. When the skyrocketing price of gold ignited a rebirth of the California gold rush, Ed purchased property in the "mother lode" country, determined to strike it rich. For two months he worked eighteen-hour days, but found nothing but dirt and rocks. Then he discovered yellow ore. He thought he had hit a bonanza. He rushed the ore to the assayer's office and began planning to hire more men and to take a European vacation.

But to Ed's consternation, the assayer announced that the ore he had mined was fool's gold. Ed could not believe it. He was sure the man had made a mistake. But no matter how vigorously Ed protested, he could not dispute the putrid sulfur smell which rose from the furnace. The ore itself settled the issue.

A miner must be certain that his find *is* gold before he can use it to acquire goods and services. So it is with God. He demands that we *be* disciples of Christ before He can use us to do His work.

So how do you know if you are a disciple of Christ? How do you know if you have experienced self-death and are worthy of reproduction? The indisputable evidence in discerning whether you are a spiritual version of fool's gold or the real thing is the presence of a Christ-like character. If Christ's character is missing, you have not died to yourself and are not fit for reproduction.

Perhaps the most difficult hurdle you will face is to really believe that your character is more important than your skills or abilities. This is so foreign to the world that even when you become committed to self-death, you will find it alien.

I had a great struggle with this. For years I had listened to preachers employ every emotional tactic imaginable to induce people to accept Christ. Some begged the congregation, suggesting that they would be doing Christ a favor by following Him. Others issued such broad invitations that no honest person should have been left in the pews. They urged everyone who had thought a bad thought, had entertained an impure motive or had broken one biblical teaching to come forward. They preached as if God would judge them according to the number of people who responded to their pleas, rather than on their Christ-like compassion for men.

So I assumed that the more people I led to Christ, the more valuable I was. I tried to attract people to Christian meetings with gimmicks that prostituted the gospel: pie-throwing contests, water-balloon fights and even haunted houses. I worked hard to polish my presentation of the plan of salvation and to refine the invitations I used after preaching. Small responses to my altar calls embarrassed me. I had a worth-by-works mentality.

I always knew in my mind that only God's Spirit moved

people to repentance and confession, and that I was called merely to testify, not to convert. But I acted as if the quality of my Christian life and the salvation of others depended on my skill and creativity in evangelism.

Finally, the Bible alerted me to the truth. First and foremost God wanted me to have the character of Christ—to *be* Christian. Only then would He work through me for His glory.

What a disarming revelation! I had mistaken activity and the response of man for righteousness. I had substituted busyness for worship. Suddenly my security in good works was devastated.

The truth was painfully obvious. One had to first *be* a doctor before he could treat the sick. One had to *be* a lawyer before he could practice law. So of course I had to *be* Christ-like before I could do the work of Christ.

Christian character consists of the combination of mental and ethical qualities that enable you to "walk in a manner worthy of the God who calls you into His own kingdom and glory" (1 Thessalonians 2:12). It exhibits the fruit of the Spirit: love, joy, peace, patience, kindness, goodness, faithfulness, gentleness and self-control (Galatians 5:22,23).

A careful examination of Christ's ministry reveals that among those virtues which epitomized His life, four qualities distinguished Him from every other person as God's only begotten Son. They were obedience, submission, love and prayer.

When I first discovered this I was stunned. Could it be that God incarnate chose to build His Church on the foundation of these four qualities? They seemed characteristic of a weak person—one who depends totally on another for direction, motivation and confidence.

But that was exactly it. These qualities perfectly described Christ's relationship to the Father. Christ's strength came from His dependence upon the Almighty. And if I were to be used by God, my relationship with Him would have to be patterned after my Lord's. Christian character is built by my willing (exercising my will) to conform every aspect of my life to the image of Christ.

Some believers have sought to join our discipling ministry with the condition that their talents be used. But such a perspective is a denial of self-death and indicates that their values are warped. A disciple's main concern ought to be that his character will be built and reproduced. A Doctor of Philosophy, a Master of Divinity or a social worker is not necessarily more valuable to a missions organization like World Impact. He is treated no differently than anyone else. We all strive to make disciples, but we know this is impossible without first being a disciple. We must know God before we can make Him known.

A disciple employs any gift or talent that builds the kingdom or edifies the body. He confidently refrains from exercising abilities that might destructively foster his pride or hinder his Christian maturity. A dead man's focus is on God. He seeks to be like Christ.

If any man had a reason to find security in his reputation, abilities or credentials it was the Apostle Paul. Yet he realized that these were rubbish compared to becoming like Christ (Philippians 3:8). A person's skill is worthless without a godly character. Of course, no mortal can achieve such qualities on his own power. But God has predestined disciples "to become conformed to the image of His Son . . ." (Romans 8:29).

One day I was sailing off the California coast with a friend when an unexpected, heavy fog rolled in and virtually wiped out all visibility. We were afraid we would never make it back to the harbor. We floated for about forty-five minutes in the fog bank, when suddenly we heard the faint but distinct tone of a foghorn. By fixing our course on that welcome sound and moving ever so carefully toward it, we eventually returned safely to the harbor. Had we not heard the foghorn we would have drifted aimlessly in the ocean.

If you have no target for your life, you are likely to drift without direction. If you aim at nothing, you will probably hit it. That is why you must thoroughly understand who Christ wants you to *be*.

Obedience, submission, love and prayer are the objectives for which you and every disciple you lead must strive. They serve as the barometer by which you can measure your growth and the progress of those whom you disciple. They are so important that we will examine them individually in the following chapters.

Disciple's Checklist—*How Do You Know If You Are a Disciple?*

☐ My Christ-like character is evidence of my self-death (being a disciple).

☐ My character is more important than my skills or abilities.

4
Obedience

Obedience is the first distinctive of a disciple. We obey God because He is the sovereign Lord of the universe and our obedience is the only acceptable response to His unspeakable kindness (Romans 2:4).

Jesus said, "If you love Me, you will keep My commandments" (John 14:15). Only those who obey God's Word demonstrate their love for Him. Your love for Christ caused you to obey His command to repent and follow Him. Your baptism, which graphically confirmed your self-death and the enthronement of Christ as the Lord of your life, was a further step of obedience (Romans 6:3,4). And the Christian life is a continuing pilgrimage of obedience.

Several years ago I visited a military base. I was impressed by the obedience that the enlisted men displayed toward their sergeant. When he told them to run, they ran. When he told them to clean the toilets, they scrubbed. There was no debate, no hesitancy—only immediate action.

The enlisted men obeyed their sergeant because he obeyed the lieutenant, who, via the chain of command, obeyed the general. Had the enlisted men refused to obey the sergeant, they would have defied the general's authority and been subject to severe consequences. Their continued well-being depended upon their obedience.

I realized that in the military the motivation for obedience is often fear, while the Christian's motivation is love. Nevertheless, the military example illustrates an important principle for believers: our welfare is a direct result of our obedience.

We are empowered to consistently obey God through our knowledge of Scripture and our surrendered will.

You Must Know God's Word

"Blessed . . . are those who hear the word of God and obey it" (Luke 11:28 NIV). It is audacious to believe that you might possibly obey God without first knowing His will.

It is unfair to punish a child for not doing what you want if you never tell him what you expect. God, however, is not unreasonable. He has clearly revealed His will for us through His Word. Therefore we must study the Bible (2 Timothy 2:15), understanding that it trains us in righteousness and teaches us how to live in a manner that is pleasing to God (2 Timothy 3:16).

The Bible does reveal God's will. But, as most of us know, Bible study is hard work. To glean its truth, we must study the Word diligently, rather than just leisurely browse through it. Many Christians remain biblically illiterate and deprive themselves of spiritual sustenance, motivation and blessing because they are too lazy to *study* God's Word.

A few years ago I became convicted about being overweight and out of shape. So I made a commitment before God and to my family that I would run every day. I knew jogging would improve my health. At first it was pure misery. There was seldom a day that I wanted to run. I could always think of countless reasons why I should skip braving that cold or wet morning—just for one day. But by will, I forced myself to keep this commitment.

Then I started to lose weight and to feel better. And the running became easier. Eventually, I lost forty-five pounds!

I must admit that I still fight running; my emotions still rationalize that I can put it off until tomorrow. But I know better, and to this day I continue to jog.

I have found many parallels between studying God's Word and running. The most difficult part of each activity is to begin. But once I start, I really enjoy both. And when I'm through, I am pleased that I have done them. I am better off for the effort. In each discipline my emotions offer several reasons why I "legitimately" could put it off just one day. However, if I miss one day, it becomes easier to justify my procrastination the next. When I do them regularly, my strength builds and they become less difficult. The disciple wills to study God's Word.

Jesus said, ". . . If you abide in My word [that is, continue daily], then you are truly disciples of Mine" (John 8:31). Consuming God's Word must be a priority in the disciple's life so "that the man of God may be adequate, equipped for every good work" (2 Timothy 3:17). You must always be "ready to make a defense to every one who asks you to give an account for the hope that is in you. . ." (1 Peter 3:15).

The experiences of biblical characters are recorded as examples for your instruction (1 Corinthians 10:11). You must continually discover scriptural principles and apply them to your life (Psalms 119:7,8).

I am convinced that there is a guiding principle or a direct command in God's Word for every decision I need to make. So if I do not know God's will in a particular situation, more than likely it is because I do not know God's Word.

When someone seeks my advice regarding an important decision, my first questions are: "Have you studied the Word? Have you listened to God Himself?" I am amazed by people who ask my counsel before they seek God's. We need the counsel of godly people who know both us and the Bible well, but this should *follow* our study of applicable biblical principles and prayer.

When confronted with a serious dilemma, a severe temptation or a momentous decision, only the naive believe they can quickly pray to God, open the Bible and magically discover the answer. While God is not limited, the Holy Spirit usually chooses to bring to our memory those things that are already there. Jesus warned, ". . . Ye do err, not knowing the scriptures, nor the power of God" (Matthew 22:29 KJV). The disciple must have a working knowledge of God's Word.

One schoolteacher believed that God was directing her to break her teaching contract in order to minister with us. She was confident that this was God's will because she had a "peace" about it.

I am always excited about new missionaries joining us in the ghetto. Our present staff cannot possibly respond to all the people who are seeking to know God through our ministry. But I knew it was not God's will for this teacher to break her contract. God says, "If a man makes a vow to the Lord, or takes an oath to bind himself with a binding obligation, he shall not violate his word; he shall do according to all that proceeds out of his mouth" (Numbers 30:2). God's Word, not "a sense of peace," reveals His will. Remember Jonah? He had no "peace" about going to Nineveh, but it was definitely God's will, as revealed by "The word of the Lord" (Jonah 1:1).

I believe that this teacher sincerely desired to obey God and that her feelings led her to believe she was correct. But the Christian life is based on obedience to God's Word, not on following your emotions. Paul said, ". . . in evil be babes, but in your thinking be mature" (1 Corinthians 14:20). "Childlike faith" is not license for ignorance. Paul said repeatedly, "I would not have you be ignorant. . . ."

Without an adequate knowledge of God's Word, a disciple is gambling his future on feelings, hopes and opinions, instead of securing it in God's will and the facts of his faith.

A disciple experiences the discovery of Jeremiah: "Thy words were found and I ate them, and Thy words became for me a joy and the delight of my heart ..." (Jeremiah 15:16).

You Must Will to Obey

You must be *committed* to obeying God's Word even before you know what it says. Years ago a well-known tight-rope-walker was about to cross Niagara Falls on a wire. He asked the crowd if they thought he could do it. When they affirmed their belief, he asked them again, "Do you really believe I can do it?" When their shouts indicated absolute faith, he asked for a volunteer to ride on his back.

Commitment is binding yourself to a person, an ideal or a goal no matter what the consequences. Your commitment is a pledge to be bound to Christ, to become one with Him; to place your future, your very life in His hands. Paul urges believers "to present your bodies a living and holy sacrifice, acceptable to God ..." (Romans 12:1).

Most Christians *want* to obey God's Word, but wanting is not enough. Wanting is often a function of your emotions. It fluctuates with your feelings. The disciple *wills* to obey God's Word.

God does not expect you to exercise a Christ-like will on your own. Paul teaches that "... it is God who is at work in you, both to will and to work for His good pleasure" (Philippians 2:13). Your Spirit-empowered will can overrule your feelings and lead you to act upon your prior commitment to Christ (Romans 8).

I recall staying at a hotel that had a swimming pool with a high diving board. With considerable trepidation I decided to venture one dive off that high board. Carefully I maneuvered my way up the metal steps to the top of the ladder and stood trembling on that slab of fiber glass. I had no doubt that gravity could pull me into the pool. But I also knew it was unlikely to do so unless I jumped. One can compare gravity to God's work of empowering us; it is always available when we choose to obey.

A prominent philosophy today is, "If it feels good, do it." Avoiding negative feelings or experiences has become the highest law for many. They mistakenly assume that pleasure and happiness are synonymous. Satan is a master at making evil look good. He paints wickedness with enticing beauty and promises delightful gratification. If sins were not pleasurable, they would be no temptation.

A man who had just left his wife in order to find happiness assured me that God would approve. God wanted him to be happy and that was impossible in his present situation—in spite of that pledge "for better or for worse . . . till death do us part." He may find temporary pleasure, but he will not find happiness. True happiness can only be found by obeying God.

When there is a conflict between God's Word and one's feelings, a disciple wills to do what God says. That is what Christianity is all about.

One of the great tragedies of twentieth-century Christianity is that many biblically knowledgeable believers are educated beyond their obedience. Some Christians exercise the "dip and skip" method of obeying Scripture. They dip into the promises and skip the commands! Or they emphasize certain "important" verses and ignore others, discrediting 2 Timothy 3:16, which declares *"All* Scripture is inspired by God . . ." (*italics added*).

My initial relationships with young men in Watts were characterized by arguments and long discussions about questions like: "Can you prove there is a God?", "How could a virgin bear a child?", or "Why would a God of love allow poverty or child abuse?"

I knew that God's Word said, "Don't get involved in arguing over unanswerable questions and controversial theological ideas ... for this kind of thing isn't worthwhile; it only does harm" (Titus 3:9 LB). But I figured this was the only way to persuade those street dudes to believe in Christ. So I skipped this principle. I was sincere in trying to convert them, but I was not obeying God's Word. And I never won an argument.

Finally, I decided to try God's way. I would not argue or defend the Bible, just proclaim it (2 Timothy 4:2). I started to pray for those young men. When the opportunity arose, I shared God's love with them. Before long God's Spirit convicted four of them to follow Christ. But the others never did. Their hearts were hardened by our debates. Christ had become a joke; Christianity, a game.

I could have avoided impeding the work of the Holy Spirit had I simply obeyed God, absolutely and without question. I had no right to choose what I would obey. Knowing what the Bible says without obeying it is a detestable affront to God.

Romans 6:16 asks, "Do you not know that when you present yourselves to someone as slaves for obedience, you are slaves of the one whom you obey. . . ?" Since the believer is committed to obeying God's will as the Holy Spirit reveals it, he studies the Word of God with a prior commitment to live what he learns. This determination is indisputable evidence that he is a disciple of Christ.

Disciple's Checklist—*Obedience*
☐ I faithfully study God's Word.
☐ I *will* to obey God's Word.

5

Submission

Joyful submission is the second mark of a disciple. Submission is much more than obedience. It is an inner attitude of trust in your sovereign, loving and omniscient God.

During my first year in Watts, I was walking down 103rd Street with three teenage friends. Suddenly one of the guys yelled, "Hit the ground!" A second guy shoved me down just as a bullet screamed over my head.

I was shaken. As I brushed myself off, I asked these guys how they knew a bullet was going to be fired, especially since it came from behind us. One of them grinned at me and quipped, "You mean you've got an education from UCLA and you don't know the sound of a gun cocking?"

I was grateful for their expertise and from then on I was happy to submit to their leadership in surviving on the streets. They never had to tell me something twice. Their word was law. I trusted them.

Christ invites us to trust Him: "Come to Me, all who are weary and heavy-laden, and I will give you rest. Take My yoke upon you, and learn from Me, for I am gentle and humble in heart; and you shall find rest for your souls. For My yoke is easy, and My load is light" (Matthew 11:28–30).

"Take My yoke" means to submit to Christ's authority, to trust Him. Submission is the precondition for the rest

Christ promises His disciples.

When I began driving a car, I grudgingly observed the speed limit. My motivation for obeying the law, however, was not trust, but fear. I did not want to get a ticket and face the consequences of paying a fine and higher insurance rates. The state was satisfied with my compliance with its authority, regardless of my motivation.

But Christ is not pleased with obedience alone; He also wants His disciples to be submissive—to trust Him. There is a great difference between submission and obedience.

The Pharisees provide a classic example of *obedience without submission.* They obeyed the letter of the Law without understanding the spirit by which God intended it to be interpreted. They did not trust the judgment of God because His higher law of love was foreign to them.

The Bible also records incidents of *submission without obedience.* If the laws of men conflict with the laws of God, the disciple can still maintain a submissive spirit by openly demonstrating his trust in God.

Peter and John maintained a submissive spirit toward God even while they disobeyed an unjust law. When those in authority over the apostles commanded them to stop teaching about Jesus, they refused to obey (Acts 4:18–20). They resumed their teaching about Christ and even prayed for boldness in doing so. Their submission to God's supreme authority required that they disobey their temporal authorities.

Please note that Peter and John did not hide their disobedience, but preached openly, trusting God with the consequences. They were willing to suffer further punishment if the authorities so ruled, knowing that their public obedience to God would bring Him glory.

Had the apostles felt guilt if someone "caught" them doing what they believed was right, they would not have had a submissive spirit. An act done with a submissive spirit causes no guilt. If a disciple openly disobeys temporal authorities in direct obedience to God's will, like Daniel's unlawful prayer (Daniel 6:10), and is willing to suffer the consequences, he is submissive.

In the 1960s many Christians participated in nonviolent protests against the unjust laws of racial discrimination. They knew that all men were made in the image of God and that dignity is our birthright. Black believers sat illegally in seats reserved for white bus riders and boldly requested service in white restaurants. They openly defied the civil authorities by obeying a higher law. Throughout their demonstrations these Christians remained submissive to God—free of guilt and willing to suffer the consequences.

A disciple strives to maintain an attitude of trust in God's authority no matter what the cost. Four biblical truths guide him in this pursuit.

Christ's Authority Is Supreme

Jesus said, "If anyone comes to Me, and does not hate his own father and mother and wife and children and brothers and sisters, yes, and even his own life, he cannot be My disciple. Whoever does not carry his own cross and come after Me cannot be My disciple" (Luke 14:26,27). Christ's use of *hatred* here refers to the authority to which a person submits, not to natural affection. Your submission to Christ, your trust in Him, must be so great that by comparison your allegiance to conflicting authorities is like hatred. Submitting so completely to Christ's authority is unreasonable for anyone but a dead man—that is, one who has made Christ the Lord of his life.

People in the inner city are often confronted with conflicting authorities. Hattie is the mother of several of our Bible club children. They live in extreme poverty, often going without food or sufficient clothing. As we met the physical needs of this family in Christ's name, Hattie came

50 *The Making of a Disciple*

to love Jesus and obeyed His command to follow Him.

Her husband was a "mule," a transporter of narcotics from Mexico to Southern California. Frequently, he forced Hattie and their children to assist him. He would strap a package of heroin to Hattie's leg, concealing it beneath her dress. Or he would attach it to his children under their clothing. He threatened to beat or even kill his family if they refused to obey. Motivated by fear of physical abuse, of which they had frequently been victims, they obeyed.

When Hattie accepted Christ, she faced a severe crisis. She knew she was disobeying God by breaking the law of the land and by endangering her children. But if she refused to obey her husband, the consequences would be dreadful.

Which authority takes precedence? To whom should she submit, Christ or her husband? Jesus left no doubt. Christ's authority is supreme (Matthew 23:10). So, risking her own life and those of her children, Hattie obeyed Christ, took up her "cross" and followed Him.

As I struggled to understand what it meant for me to trust God, Luke 14:33 hit home: "So no one can become my disciple unless he first sits down and counts his blessings—and then renounces them *all* for me" (LB, *italics added*). When I listed my blessings, all of the things I count dear—my wife, my children, my work, my health, my friends, my reputation, my home—I realized that any one of these could be my god. I had to admit that if God chose to take one or all of these away, I would face a real crisis.

But then God reminded me that I was a dead man. And a dead man has no possessions. I relinquished all rights to these blessings when Christ became the Lord of my life. Now He is simply loaning them to me. If God chooses in His divine wisdom to remove one or all of these things I count so dear, I believe that He knows best and will give me the grace to continue to delight in Him.

Some believers attach qualifiers to their obedience, like,

"I'll go anywhere for you, God—except Watts," or "I'll do anything you ask, Lord—if you guarantee no harm will come to my wife." What this really means is, "I won't go anywhere or do anything, Lord—unless I okay it."

Whenever we place a stipulation on our obedience to God, we completely deny our trust in Him. Any reservation about submitting to God discloses that we think we can take better care of ourselves than God can, that God does not know what is best for us. How foolish! Anything less than joyful submission is a denial of God's supreme authority, wisdom and love, and of our self-death.

Christ Rules Today Through Delegated Authority

Jesus declared, ". . . *All* authority has been given to Me in heaven and on earth." On this basis He commissioned His disciples to "Go . . . and make disciples of all the nations. . . ." Implicit in this command was the investment of *His* authority in His disciples to build and regulate His Church, for He said to do it "in the name of the Father and the Son and the Holy Spirit" (Matthew 28:18,19).

Jesus told His disciples, "He who receives you receives Me, and he who receives Me receives Him who sent Me" (Matthew 10:40). Here was the chain of authority: Christ represented the Father; the apostles represented Christ. To receive an apostle was to receive the Father (John 13:20); to reject an apostle was to reject Christ and the Father.

The Apostle Paul frequently referred to his God-given authority: "For even if I should boast somewhat further about our authority, which the Lord gave for building you up and not for destroying you, I shall not be put to shame" (2 Corinthians 10:8). And often Paul exercised his authority: "Now we command you, brethren, in the name of our Lord Jesus Christ . . ." (2 Thessalonians 3:6).

The first disciples delegated the authority they received from Christ to those they trained. With Christ's authority they appointed Church leaders (Acts 6:3,6; 14:23) and commissioned them to instruct others, who in turn would teach others (2 Timothy 2:2).

Paul entrusted his authority to Titus (Titus 1:5) and instructed him to "speak to the Christians there as sternly as necessary to make them strong in the faith ..." (Titus 1:13 LB) and to correct them "as one who has every right to do so ..." (Titus 2:15 LB).

Paul expected the Christians to submit to the authority of two of his disciples just as they would to Christ Himself: "Please follow their instructions and do everything you can to help them as well as *all* others like them who work hard at your side with such real devotion" (1 Corinthians 16:16 LB, *italics added*). In the New Testament Church, second- and third-generation disciples freely exercised authority.

Since all authority comes from God (Romans 13:1–5) and He gives authority to those whom He chooses (Ephesians 4:11,12), our attitude toward those in whom He entrusts authority reflects our real attitude toward God. Whenever His delegated authority touches our lives, Christ requires us to acknowledge it and joyfully submit to it just as we would to Christ Himself. Our submission is a declaration of our trust in God.

You Receive Authority Through Submission

The authority a person exercises is determined by the authority to which he submits. The Roman centurion knew that if Christ spoke one word, his servant would be healed. The centurion explained his confidence: "For I also am a man set under authority ..." (Luke 7:7,8 KJV). He understood the power vested in delegated authority. As long as he was in submission to his leaders, every command he uttered carried the authority of the Roman emperor. To disobey him was to demean the emperor. The centurion's authority was great because of whom he represented.

The centurion recognized this same principle in Christ. Since He represented God, and was completely submissive to the Father's will, every word Jesus uttered was invested with God's authority (Ephesians 1:20–23). The centurion's confession, "I also am a man set under authority," capsulizes the scriptural basis for all true authority: a person who is not in submission has no right to exercise authority.

One day I saw a massive traffic jam in downtown Los Angeles. A man was standing in the middle of a busy intersection stopping traffic at will, first from one direction, then another. Finally he stopped traffic coming from all four directions.

The motorists were furious. Bystanders were yelling. I didn't know what to make of it. The man looked competent. He was well dressed, clean shaven and apparently not a bit disturbed by the ruckus he was causing. But I could not figure out his motives. There was no fire, no accident, no injury.

When the police arrived and escorted the man to the curb, the crowd jeered and hollered, "Throw him in the nuthouse! Take him to a psychiatrist!" They had passed judgment on the man and were ready to commit him to an institution because he had obviously exercised an authority that was not his. He was not a policeman or a fireman. He was simply a citizen—trying to find his contact lens! The crowd concluded that anyone who would exercise authority without being under authority must be insane.

A Christian has no authority unless it comes from Christ. And since Christ rules through delegated authority, when we refuse to submit to those in authority over us, we lose our authority. We find an instance of this when John instructed Gaius not to obey Diotrephes, because Diotrephes did not obey John (3 John 9–11).

Unwillingness to submit to those in authority over us is a great sin with severe consequences. Paul writes, "And if anyone does not obey our instruction in this letter, take special note of that man and do not associate with him, so that he may be put to shame. And yet do not regard him as an enemy, but admonish him as a brother" (2 Thessalonians 3:14,15).

A believer who refuses to submit to those in authority over him is like a runaway child. He will try to fend for himself, but without adult supervision his survival is in serious jeopardy. One who deprives himself of a spiritual guardian's protective custody rejects God's provision for his nurture and faces a tenuous future. Trust is a disciple's strength (Isaiah 30:15).

When I started ministering in Watts I was not in submission to anyone. Soon I realized that without being under the authority of godly men, I had no authority. That was bad for me, but worse for those to whom I ministered.

I prayed diligently for a group of men to whom I could submit, because "in the multitude of counsellors there is safety" (Proverbs 11:14 KJV). And I knew that God had spoken to early Church leaders corporately (Acts 15:28).

First John 4:1 says to "test the spirits" before submitting. This is a command to seek the leadership of godly people. I recognized that these men had to meet certain biblical requirements in order to receive God's authority. Both individually and corporately they needed to submit to God's Word as their absolute authority (1 Timothy 6:3–5; 2 Timothy 3:16,17). They needed to have proven their Christian commitment (2 Corinthians 8:22) by serving others (Matthew 20:26,27) and by being faithful in all things, like their stewardship of money (Luke 16:10–12). In summary, they had to live their faith, providing a model that I could emulate (3 John 11).

And the Lord faithfully provided these men. They became the Executive Board of World Impact. Once I had verified their commitment to God, I knew I could trust

God's leadership through them to actively guide and admonish me.

When these men assumed authority over me and our ministry, I verbally affirmed my submission to them. Christians must submit to their leaders *voluntarily*. There is no biblical provision for leaders to exercise their authority over one who does not submit. That is why the New Testament speaks first to the one who is responsible to submit, and then to the person who is to exercise authority: first to the children, then to the parents; first to the wife, then to the husband; first to the servant, then to the master. Consequently, my relationship with our Board hinged upon my submission to them.

My submission does not preclude further personal responsibility to search the Scriptures and test the leadership (Acts 17:11). However, I do this with a submissive spirit, *trusting* that such study will only enhance the instruction received. If we differ on an issue, I trust that these godly leaders will be open to discussion or will appreciate any correction or enlightenment. My spirit as a searcher is not critical, rebellious or distrustful. It is submissive. I love them and honor them. And I know the reverse is also true.

Submission to godly men who know me well has alleviated a tremendous amount of pressure. On the basis of their guidance and wisdom, I can now confidently exercise authority over those who choose to submit to me. In turn, many of our staff who have been entrusted with leadership positions exercise authority over other staff members and Christians in the ghetto. Christ's delegated authority has in fact been passed on to us.

Exercising this principle has provided direction for our staff in certain tense situations. We have often been asked for money to buy food. We realized that the money we gave frequently purchased liquor or narcotics. So we decided to provide a well-balanced meal for those who said they were hungry.

This sounded good in theory, but it did not work well on the streets. When someone was offered food, he responded, "I'd rather have money. Don't you trust me?" No matter how compassionately we explained, arguments and bitter feelings resulted.

Finally, I told our staff to simply say, "My boss says we cannot give out money, but I will feed you if you want." Surprisingly, that ended our dilemma. The people who asked for money respected the authority to which our staff submitted, even if they had no idea who that authority was. They could argue with the person, but not with his authority. A disciple joyfully submits to Christ and His delegated authorities.

Disciples Exercise Their Authority Through Servanthood

Instead of using brute force or authoritarian demands, a disciple exercises his authority through servanthood. Jesus told His disciples, ". . . You know that those who are recognized as rulers of the Gentiles lord it over them; and their great men exercise authority over them. But it is not so among you . . . whoever wishes to be first among you shall be slave of all. For even the Son of Man did not come to be served, but to serve, and to give His life a ransom for many" (Mark 10:42–45).

Christ's message was plain: spiritual love serves, it does not desire. Servanthood is the highest form of leadership. The mature Christian chooses servanthood over lordship in every situation.

There are very few individuals who make such a stunning first impression that I am awed by them. One day it dawned on me that those unique people who do, have one thing in common: servanthood.

Walter is one of these remarkable people. The first time

we met, he offered to clear his calendar in order to drive me to my appointments. He was sincerely concerned about my welfare. I never imagined that he was one of the top business executives in the country.

Walter never needs to say it, but I know he will do anything in his power to serve me. If I were in a desperate situation, I would not hesitate to phone him. Servanthood permeates his life.

Jesus said, "This is My commandment, that you love one another, *just as I have loved you*" (John 15:12, *italics added*). And Christ's love for His disciples was unselfish servanthood. He voluntarily assumed the form of a slave (Philippians 2:7). He washed their feet and willingly took their place on a cross. Jesus was not screaming and kicking when they led Him to be crucified. He was compassionate and forgiving. He served without reservation and then announced, "I gave you an example that you also should do as I did to you" (John 13:15).

The apostles, whose authority in the Church was beyond question, were servant-leaders. They did not "lord it over" their spiritual children (2 Corinthians 1:24). They exercised authority in a humble, loving manner.

Unlike nonbelievers who serve because of fear, pride, loyalty or a desire for money, a disciple's motivation is love. He puts his brother's welfare above his own. Privacy is an infrequent luxury. Inconvenience is not unusual. He ministers unnoticed and in the excitement or tragedy of the moment, often leaves unthanked. Any high-handed word or action is out of character.

I remember teaching a seminar in a room where there was no stand for the blackboard. Al Ewert, our Wichita director, was with me. Quietly, completely unnoticed, Al slipped behind the blackboard and stood holding it against his body. For three hours I taught about discipleship—self-death, submission, obedience, love and servanthood. As the session ended, I looked at Al and was profoundly moved. I had talked about a Christ-like character while Al had lived it. "... whoever wishes to become great among you shall be your servant" (Matthew 20:26). Disciples exercise their authority through servanthood.

The submission-authority relationships that God ordained serve as the central nervous system for Christ's Church. We can only function correctly in the body of Christ if we understand and live by these four biblical truths which form the groundwork for joyful submission.

Disciple's Checklist—*Submission*

☐ I have an inner attitude of trust in my sovereign, loving and omniscient God.

☐ Christ's authority is supreme in my life.

☐ When God's delegated authority touches my life, I submit to it just as I would to Christ.

☐ I can exercise authority because I submit to authority.

☐ I exercise my authority through servanthood.

6

Love One Another

The third distinctive of a disciple is that he loves other Christians. Jesus said, "By this all men will know that you are My disciples, if you have love for one another" (John 13:35). Love for one another is our badge of discipleship.

Some time ago I heard a deafening noise in the lobby of my hotel. I could not imagine what was going on until I saw a very distinctive red fez. Then I noticed that almost every man's head was adorned similarly. The Shriners were in town! No one had to tell me. Their hats made them easy to recognize.

Many groups are identified by their insignia or common dress: policemen wear uniforms, Rotarians wear pins, basketball players wear jerseys. But disciples do not need to wear "one-way" pins, clerical collars or ecclesiastical robes. We can have diversity in garments and be as easy to identify as a giant in a colony of midgets. We have the most distinctive identification of all.

It is unnecessary for our staff homes in the ghetto to have signs that advertise "World Impact Home" or "House of God." Our love for one another must be so obvious that our neighbors cannot mistake our allegiance to Christ.

When some of our women's staff went to the corner market for the first time, the proprietor said, "Oh, you're from the Christian home, aren't you? I can always tell you girls by your big smile and your love."

A month after we opened a staff home in Fresno, someone who had an appointment with me lost our address as well as the name of our organization. He stopped in the community and asked a neighbor if she knew where a group of Christians lived. She replied, "Oh, yes, we all know who they are. They live on the next block on the corner." His encounter with our neighbor spoke more loudly than anything I had to say.

Since the world knows we are disciples by our love for one another, we must make sure our identity is conspicuous. In order to have a strong, consistent love for other believers, we must understand and be experiencing forgiveness and community.

Forgiveness

A disciple cannot love God or himself, let alone others, unless he accepts God's complete forgiveness and on that basis forgives himself, forgives others and accepts the forgiveness of others.

Accept God's Forgiveness

You must accept God's complete forgiveness for your past, present and future. There is no sin for which you cannot be forgiven by confession and genuine repentance. God promises to cleanse us from *all* unrighteousness (1 John 1:9) and to forget our sins forever (Isaiah 43:25). God's forgiveness is perfect.

Seven years ago Pat Williams attended her first World Impact Bible club on a vacant lot in Watts. When she made a commitment to follow Jesus, her life began to change. She faithfully studied the Bible, prayed and worshipped God. After graduation she joined our staff and started to minister in the very community in which she had grown up. Pat appeared to be a sterling example of God's redemptive power.

But hidden under her contagious smile, Pat concealed a childhood devastated by oppression and physical abuse. Her father deserted the family when her mother was three months pregnant with Pat. She and her five brothers had three different fathers. They lived in poverty, at times going without food.

But it was the sexual abuse that haunted Pat. Her own uncle began raping her when she was still a child. "He'd give me candy," Pat relates, "and come get me whenever he pleased. Since he was part of the family, there was nothing I could do about it. He threatened to kill me if I ever told anyone."

Pat grew up hating all men and hating herself for what her uncle had done to her. Even after she joined our staff, she detested the sight of men or having to be with them. Her Christian life was crippled by guilt, hate and hurt. Like so many Christians, Pat had accepted God's gift of salvation, but had not accepted His complete forgiveness.

Forgive Yourself on the Basis of God's Forgiveness of You

You demonstrate that you have accepted God's complete forgiveness by forgiving yourself. When you understand that God loves you, your sense of spiritual dignity is restored. This liberates you to forgive yourself. Only then can you love and accept who you are. Paul, both the "chief of sinners" and the great apostle of Christ, declares, "But by the grace of God I am what I am . . ." (1 Corinthians 15:10). Divine approval is the fabric of self-love.

Paul indicates the quality of self-love God expects from disciples. "No one hates his own body but lovingly cares for it, just as Christ cares for his body the church . . ."

(Ephesians 5:29 LB). Christ intended that you have a healthy, positive opinion of yourself. The very repetition of the biblical teaching, "love your neighbor as yourself," underscores the importance God places on self-love. If you do not love yourself, it will invariably surface in a lack of love for your neighbor.

Failure to forgive yourself when God has forgiven you relegates God's forgiveness to an abstract idea. It means that you do not believe that His forgiveness for your sins was perfect. You question His sovereignty by denying the effectiveness of Christ's saving and healing work. Your pride says that your sins are too great for God to forgive and that you are beyond His redemption.

This renders your Christian life a shambles. It robs you of the peace, security and love God intended for you to enjoy. The absence of these experiences is destructive, not redemptive. No disciple who is dead to himself and has Christ living in him would contemplate doing less than forgiving himself because God has forgiven him.

Pat Williams realized that self-hatred was foreign to a disciple. But even though she had been the *victim* of sexual abuse, she felt guilty and dirty. How could God forgive her? How could she forgive herself?

When Pat moved into our women's staff home, she experienced the security of God's unconditional love. Through acceptance in the body, she realized that God loved her no matter what she had done or what had happened to her. Because of Christ's sacrifice, God erased her sins and paid for the abuse. He treated her as if they had never existed. On that basis she could love herself.

Pat says it best: "I found out that when Jesus died, He paid for all the hurt, guilt and bitterness in my life. He took care of that. By worrying about the past and not accepting God's perfect forgiveness, I was questioning His power to completely clean me and make me new. But now I know He has completely forgiven me, and so I can accept and forgive myself."

Forgive Others

Once you have been forgiven, you must forgive others. Jesus taught, "For if you forgive men for their transgressions, your heavenly Father will also forgive you. But if you do not forgive men, then your Father will not forgive your transgressions" (Matthew 6:14,15). Christ's prayer reflects this vital union: "And forgive us our sins, for we ourselves also forgive everyone who is indebted to us . . ." (Luke 11:4). You forgive in gratitude to God for His forgiveness of you, not in order to earn your forgiveness. Forgiving others verifies that you have been forgiven.

You cannot receive God's forgiveness without giving it to others. When our boys were infants, the doctor told us that he could inoculate them for every disease except chicken pox. If they came in contact with a child who had this disease, they were bound to contract it themselves. Forgiveness is like chicken pox. If you have it, you will give it to others.

Forgiving others is a hallmark of the Christian faith. Jesus forgave us, for whose sins He was crucified, while He still hung on the cross (Luke 23:34). Stephen forgave those who were stoning him even as the rocks crushed his body (Acts 7:60). Paul summarizes the Christian position: "And be kind to one another, tender-hearted, forgiving each other, just as God in Christ also has forgiven you" (Ephesians 4:32). Your forgiveness of others must be wholehearted, patterned after God's forgiveness of you.

Forgiving another person is a miracle of God. It is His work, not yours. Even with a willing heart, the pain is sometimes so severe that you simply cannot believe that forgiving and forgetting are possible. But because of God's forgiveness of you and the grace that He provides, you can forgive.

If you are hurt by someone but repress the pain instead of dealing with it through forgiveness, the guilt, bitterness and anxiety remain to aggravate the discord. This seriously jeopardizes your emotional health by dampening the peace of God and the joy of the Christian life. The negative emotions bottled inside eat away at you like a cancer.

Any failure to joyfully forgive others discloses an ignorance of God's gracious provision for you. You become like the ungrateful servant in Matthew 18:21-35, readily enjoying the release purchased by divine mercy, but cruelly denying similar grace to others.

Understandably, Pat Williams harbored hatred for her uncle and resentment for her mother. How could they have allowed a child to experience such perversion? Somehow Christ's teaching, "forgive, and ye shall be forgiven" (Luke 6:37 KJV) did not make much sense.

But when Pat fully accepted God's forgiveness, He replaced the piercing hurt and insidious guilt of her past with a deep security in His love. This produced a very delightful self-love. After experiencing such a perfect forgiveness, how could Pat do less than forgive her uncle and mother? Forgiving others is following Christ's example.

Accept the Forgiveness of Others

Colossians 3:13 urges us to forgive one another because Christ forgives us. Forgiving *one another* requires us to accept, as well as give, forgiveness. Accepting forgiveness usually follows our earnest request for forgiveness. However, sometimes people offer to forgive us for wrongs that we thought were so extreme that we did not even dare to ask for their forgiveness. We may find it hard to believe that they sincerely want to forgive us.

But when someone forgives you, you must be quick to accept. Failure to do this is sin. It indicates that you believe your offense against this person was so great that God's power is insufficient to enable him to forgive. It denies Christ's perfect atonement in *his* life. Not accepting a person's forgiveness will offend him and damage your relationship with him. It prolongs the hurt and division between you. Further, it might cause him to stumble in the future by withholding forgiveness from others, since your rejection could lead him to believe that it would not be accepted anyway.

One day Pat's uncle may accept God's forgiveness and learn that Pat has already forgiven him. He may, however, be so overwhelmed by the wretched nature of his sins against Pat that he feels unable to accept her forgiveness. But in obedience to God, he must.

Pat's uncle certainly knows about the resentment and bitterness Pat had against him. Were he to accept Pat's forgiveness and then to forgive Pat for her negative emotions, God would want Pat to joyfully accept his forgiveness.

While accepting forgiveness is important, your healing does not depend on another person's giving or accepting forgiveness. It is a result of God's perfect provision through Christ's atonement.

Accepting and giving forgiveness break down the walls which obstruct relationships. When there are no barriers between people, love for one another is the only remaining alternative.

Community

You cannot experience true Christianity in isolation. God Himself is a community of three persons, constantly interrelating in an intimate way. Since you were created in the image of God, the more closely you conform to the Godhead the more abundant your life will be. You can only realize the fullness of your humanity in healthy relationships.

Jesus recognized the necessity of relationships. His initial act of ministry was to call twelve men to "be with Him" (Mark 3:14). He formed a community. It was from this context that He taught His disciples how to maintain lasting and intimate relationships with both God and man: to love the Lord with all your heart—and your neighbor as yourself.

Community Is Your Primary Link With God

Christ is the Head of the body (Ephesians 1:22,23) and God is the Head of Christ (1 Corinthians 11:3). If you are not part of a Christian body, you are outside of God's corporate, creative purpose for His people and you lose your most vital link with God.

The Holy Spirit repeatedly uses the functioning of the human body as a visual aid to explain how Christians should relate to Christ and to each other. Our understanding of Christian community is heightened by drawing parallels between the body of Christ and our physical body.

There has never been an instance of a foot being connected to a head apart from the body. It is a physical impossibility. Similarly, no Christian can have an exclusive attachment to God. "For the body is not one member, but many" (1 Corinthians 12:14). A believer relates to the Head through the body.

I will never forget watching a chicken rancher chop off the head of a chicken. When the head fell to the ground, the rest of the chicken ran frantically in circles. Dust flew. Feathers scattered. Then, suddenly, the body collapsed.

A Christian severed from the Head can appear to be alive for a while. But he will soon collapse because there is only one way to draw nourishment and direction from the Head—and that is to be part of a body (*see* Colossians 2:19 NIV). A Christian without community is like a chicken with its head cut off. Christian community is your primary lifeline to God.

Community Is Your Link With Other Believers

How can a disciple obey Christ's command to "love one another" without others who can be the object of his love? No Christian can be healthy without other Christians. That is why every believer immediately enters the body upon conversion. "Now you are Christ's body, and individually members of it. . . . For by one Spirit we were *all* baptized into one body . . ." (1 Corinthians 12:27,13, *italics added*).

Positionally, every Christian is a member of Christ's redeemed community. The Bible never addresses the possibility of position without function. Attempting to live the Christian life without a practical relationship to the body is risky speculation at best. Consequently, it is a top priority for every disciple to belong to a healthy, functioning Christian body.

A *healthy* Christian body is characterized by unity. It is composed of disciples who have died to themselves and are in complete submission to Christ. They rest in the knowledge that He "has arranged the parts in the body, every one of them, just as he wanted them to be" (1 Corinthians 12:18 NIV).

The book of Acts documents the centrality of unity in the Christian Church. Early believers were a closely knit family. When Peter preached at Pentecost, the other apostles stood with him (Acts 2:14). First-century disciples learned, ate, fellowshipped and prayed together (Acts 2:42). They "had all things in common" (Acts 2:44).

No part of a healthy body can act independently. My daily jogging would be greatly impaired if my legs refused to cooperate with each other. If my right leg insisted on going forward while my left leg went backward, I would fall flat on my face.

The words and actions of each member of Christ's body must promote unity among believers. Unity is developed through fellowship; regular, honest communication; and freely giving and receiving forgiveness. A disciple is committed to sacrificing his own good for the welfare of the body because he knows that unity will bring glory to God.

Unity is both the purpose and the fruit of community. At World Impact we prepare in groups, team-teach, work, live and relax together. This strengthens our unity and enhances our Christian growth and ministry. Our students and neighbors learn much more about Christian love by watching how we relate to each other than they do by hearing what we say. The world understands God's love through our unity (John 17:21–23).

Most disunity within the body is grounded in pride. We begin to demand *our* rights and guard *our* time, forgetting that we exchanged these for peace with God when we met Christ at the cross. We seek to receive the praise of men, rather than to bring glory to God through all that we do. Jesus condemned the Pharisees "for they loved the approval of men rather than the approval of God" (John 12:43). Pride is a denial of self-death and has no place among God's people.

A dangerous form of pride is jealousy. Jealousy cripples a body which must have cooperation among all its members in order to effectively serve God. James 3:16 warns, "For where jealousy and selfish ambition exist, there is disorder and every evil thing."

I understand how jealousy could creep into a Christian body. Even this book could cause division. You see, while I am the author, I have benefited greatly from the suggestions of our directors and a few other leaders. Then five of our Los Angeles staff helped me edit it. Another four people labored selflessly in typing the manuscripts.

Any one of these contributors could say, "Look at all the work I put into that, and no one will ever know. Keith gets all the credit." Jealousy. But because these disciples know that God, not Keith, receives all the glory, jealousy is averted. God uses people broken in spirit, with humble hearts, uninterested in personal accolades, glorying only in the cross of Christ. "Behold, how good and how pleasant it is for brethren to dwell together in unity!" (Psalms 133:1 KJV).

A *functioning* Christian body seeks to stimulate maturity in all its members. Since the body is no stronger than its weakest part, its health depends on the well-being of each member. Romans 12:5 says, "so we, who are many, are one body in Christ, and individually members one of another." The relationship among the members of the body is so intimate that what affects one, affects all.

Once I went sailing with a friend in a small boat. When we returned, he asked me to keep the boat from ramming the pier by tying the boat to a metal cleat on the dock. Barefooted and eager to please, I jumped out of the boat, rope in hand. Unfortunately, my big toe tried to uproot that solidly secured cleat—but the cleat did not budge. My toe throbbed with pain. I dropped the rope and the boat crashed into the dock.

Immediately, every organ, limb and faculty of my body focused its undivided attention on the plight of my toe. My stomach was no longer concerned about lunch. My mouth did not chastise my toe for being clumsy. My hand was no longer anxious to secure the rope. My head did not care about the damage to the boat. Every part of my body was unashamedly concerned about the welfare of my toe. When my toe ached, my entire body hurt.

So it is in Christ's body. We are in such close fellowship that when one member hurts, we all hurt; when one part rejoices, we all rejoice (Romans 12:15).

A hurting Christian cannot withhold his struggles from the community. His burdens, heartaches and concerns are immediately relayed through the body to the Head, which

coordinates an appropriate response. The body promotes
health by channeling every weakness and hurt into its own
bloodstream for purification through forgiveness and healing. Only a sick body lacks this intimacy.

Members of a mature body have graduated from the in-
complete idea of "going to church" to the biblical teaching
that they *are* the Church. In Christ, disciples "are being built
together to become a dwelling in which God lives by his
Spirit" (Ephesians 2:22 NIV). No longer restrained by bricks
and mortar, the Church functions at full force in the business world, at school and in the neighborhood. Worship
ceases to be confined to Sunday morning. Every action,
word and thought is offered as worship to God.

The benefits of community for a disciple are so great that
it is almost impossible to survive without it. Where else can
a disciple be in submission to godly men who know him
well? Where else can he be nurtured and lovingly held accountable for his Christian growth and maturity? Where
else can he become like Christ by observing the lives of
others? Where else can he experience sweet and pure fellowship? Where else can he be so secure in his neighbor's
love that he is liberated to love others even as God loves
him? Where else can he belong to a chorus that with one
voice sings a continuous anthem of praise and worship to
the Creator? Where else can his witness to the world be so
bright? Where else can he *be* a disciple?

Disciple's Checklist—*Love One Another*
☐ My love for other Christians is conspicuous.
☐ I have accepted God's forgiveness for my past, present and future.
☐ I have forgiven myself, based on God's forgiveness of me.
☐ I forgive others readily.
☐ I accept the forgiveness of others.
☐ I am part of a healthy, functioning Christian community.

7
Prayer

Prayer is the fourth distinctive of a disciple. Through prayer a Christian encounters the living God. ". . . In Christ Jesus our Lord . . . we have boldness and confident access . . ." to the Father (Ephesians 3:11,12). A believer's character is fashioned by his communication with God.

Communication is the secret to every healthy relationship. It did not take long for my wife, Katie, and me to realize that our union would rise or fall according to the quality of our communication; the more deeply we shared with each other, the faster we would become one. This is not surprising, since my relationship with Katie is modeled after Christ's relationship with me (Ephesians 5:23–25). Good communication transforms acquaintances into friends and superficiality into intimacy.

The quality of my communication with Katie is enhanced if I observe four guidelines. These same principles apply to a believer's prayer life.

Compliment First

Nothing facilitates a healthy relationship more than an honest compliment. A positive, building comment is a gesture of respect and admiration.

When I come home my first words set the tempo for the entire evening. And once the direction is established, it is

73

hard to reverse. If I greet my wife with, "Can't you ever lock the gate? Don't you realize how dangerous it is with our boys outside?" you can predict the consequences. What a difference it makes when I say, "Baby, you look like a million bucks."

Katie knows that my words are an extension of my heart. There is no elixir more likely to keep the exhilaration of courtship in a marriage than praise. When I am wise enough to compliment first, our communication is healthy and building.

David realized this when he advised us how to approach God: "Enter into his gates with thanksgiving, and into his courts with praise: be thankful unto him, and bless his name" (Psalms 100:4 KJV).

Prayer is primarily an avenue for the disciple to worship and honor his God. Anticipate with excitement the opportunity of being in the presence of the King of kings. Let gratitude flow from your lips and let your very being express your awe of the Almighty. You have good reason to declare your love for God: "For the Lord is good; his mercy is everlasting; and his truth endureth to all generations" (Psalms 100:5 KJV).

Be an Active Listener

When we first got married, Katie was telling me about an alarming news story in Washington. Halfway through her description I interrupted and finished the story for her. Nothing frustrated Katie more. Although she never directly said it, I quickly realized that either that habit or her husband had to go. God used my patient wife to teach me a valuable lesson: communication is much more than talking. It is active listening, giving one's undivided attention.

Failure to listen is an insult. When Katie tells me about conversations with her friends, places she has been and things she has learned, I love her enough to become involved in her life by concentrating on what she says.

I would feel shortchanged if after I poured out my heart to God, there was no response. But the Lord promises to answer (Psalms 91:15). God desires perfect communication with His children. He speaks to me through His Word, brings Scripture to my memory, and fills my mind with His beauty, encouragement and will. I need only to heed His advice: "Cease striving and know that I am God . . ." (Psalms 46:10).

I have discovered that with God, as with Katie, our most meaningful communication occurs when we are alone. I listen best when there are no distractions—no radio, no phone, no other people. I am sure that this is what Jesus had in mind when He said to His disciples, ". . . Come away by yourselves to a lonely place and rest a while" (Mark 6:31).

Be Consistent

It is all too easy for me to come home after a long day, utter a few oft-repeated niceties, flop into a chair and read the mail—practically ignoring my dear wife. It takes real discipline to get past the trivialities and openly share new ideas, exciting plans or unusual events. It is even harder to be honest about hurts, concerns and trials with which I am struggling.

Sometimes I feel that after being bombarded with people, problems and needs all day, it is pure agony to rehearse these incidents one more time. How foolish! Katie is my greatest supporter. She wants to help carry my burdens and share my joys. Consistent communication enables us to think alike, act alike and be confident in each other. Sharing with Katie and seeking her advice affirm that I value who she is. If I fail to communicate, I exclude her from who I am, and our marriage covenant is reduced to a piece of paper.

All too often the same temptation to laziness creeps into

my prayer life. I can rationalize, "God knows anyway. I'm too tired. I haven't got the time. I'll tell Him tomorrow." As with Katie, it is easy to put off. Nobody knows. No one holds me accountable. But it is a fallacy to think that consistent communication with God is optional. If my communication is sporadic, our relationship deteriorates. First, my partner and I know. Then others. Then everyone.

Consistency in a disciple's prayer life is like endurance in a long-distance runner. There are no shortcuts to its development. It is built up over an extended period of daily practice. But unless you use it, you lose it. When you stop for a while you can not begin again where you left off.

Intimacy with God demands regular communication. If you have not talked with Him for a long time and a crisis strikes, you feel awkward and insecure in His presence. Without consistent communication, the believer faces life on very shaky footing. Regular communication with God makes your heart, your motives, your thoughts and even your instincts coincide with His. That's why 1 Thessalonians 5:17 instructs us to "pray without ceasing." Your faithfulness makes you welcome in God's presence: "Let us then approach the throne of grace with confidence, so that we may receive mercy and find grace to help us in our time of need" (Hebrews 4:16 NIV).

Be Completely Honest

At the outset of our relationship, Katie and I made a commitment to be absolutely honest with each other. We knew that our marriage would grow strong if the only surprises in it were pleasant. A relationship built on half-truths or misleading distortions is like a house of cards: it crumbles with the slightest pressure.

We discuss our finances together, budget what we can spend, agree on what we cannot afford. We concur on our social engagements and ministry activities before we make commitments.

There is never a time when Katie does not know where I am. I leave a detailed itinerary when I travel: flight numbers, arrival times, hotels, contact people, speaking engagements and appointments. She can always reach me. I phone every day when I am gone.

Our commitment to active openness not only enables us to share our needs, hurts and questions before they become frustrations, but also prevents suspicion or distrust.

Many Christians have the audacity to try to deceive their all-knowing God. They rationalize their motives, balk at confessing some of their sins or refuse to yield certain areas of their lives. David was like this. He tried to hide his sins of murder and adultery until God finally confronted him through Nathan (2 Samuel 12). But David learned his lesson. He became completely "up-front" with God: "For I acknowledge my transgressions: and my sin is ever before me" (Psalms 51:3 KJV).

God will not listen to your prayers if you try to hide your sins (Psalms 66:18). Isaiah 59:2 says, ". . . your iniquities have made a separation between you and your God, And your sins have hid His face from you, so that He does not hear." Without listening there is no communication; without communication, no relationship; without relationship, no discipleship. Absolute honesty with God is essential for the disciple.

Prayer is the disciple's most intimate channel of communication with his God. The quality of his communication determines the strength of his relationship. Prayer is both the proof and the unquestioned priority of one who pursues God (Luke 18:1).

Disciple's Checklist—*Prayer*
My prayer life is characterized by:
☐ Complimenting God first.
☐ Actively listening.
☐ Consistency.
☐ Complete honesty.

SECTION III

How Do You Make Disciples?

8

Created to Reproduce

Once you have died to yourself, you are a disciple. And disciples are made to reproduce. Jesus was unequivocal: "... If a man remains in me ... he *will bear much fruit* ..." (John 15:5 NIV, *italics added*). There is no higher calling, no clearer commission in the New Testament than to reproduce in others the character that God's Spirit has created in you. Christ expects every Christian to bear spiritual fruit.

Paul reveals the significance of having healthy spiritual children: "For what is our hope, our joy, or the crown in which we will glory in the presence of our Lord Jesus when he comes? *Is it not you?* Indeed, you are our glory and joy" (1 Thessalonians 2:19,20 NIV, *italics added*).

Paul knew that simply leading a person to Christ was not enough. He regarded his labors to be in vain if his spiritual children did not become mature disciples. And mature disciples reproduce their lives in others—they bear lasting fruit. Note that Paul was writing to believers whom *he* had led to the Lord when he urged them to hold "fast the word of life, so that in the day of Christ I may have cause to glory because I did not run in vain nor toil in vain" (Philippians 2:16). He repeated this concern in 1 Thessalonians 3:5: "... when I could stand it no longer, I sent to find out about your faith. I was afraid that in some way the tempter might have tempted you and our efforts might have been useless" (NIV).

And to the Galatian believers he wrote, "I fear for you, that perhaps I have labored over you in vain" (Galatians 4:11).

How could Paul dare to suggest that his renowned missionary journeys might have been wasted when their result was so many new Christians? Why did the apostle agonize over the possibility that his flock might have become carnal or worldly? The reason is obvious. Paul knew that Jesus was uncompromising: either one dies to himself and reproduces—or he is not a follower of Christ. Jesus left no other option. Christ Himself told His disciples, ". . . I chose you *to go and bear fruit*—fruit that will last . . ." (John 15:16 NIV, *italics added*).

Only the ill-informed or immature are so preoccupied with good works that they haven't got time to nurture their spiritual children to reproduction. No mature Christian is content to be spiritually barren.

Take a moment to examine your life. Is there one person walking with God today and investing in others the fullness of life he has in Christ as a result of your ministry? One man? One woman? If not, you have been unfruitful.

Perhaps you faithfully attend church, sing in the choir, usher, sponsor a youth group or serve as an elder, deacon or even a pastor. You might witness every day or teach group Bible studies. These are commendable activities but they fall short of fulfilling your high calling to make disciples.

Activity is no substitute for obedience; busyness cannot replace reproduction. One functioning disciple is more valuable in building the Church than a host of carnal believers. Resist the temptation to be so active in "Christian work" that you neglect the business of the kingdom. Reevaluate your priorities in light of Christ's commission to make disciples.

Your commitment to discipling is engendered by your

love for God in response to Christ's unselfish sacrifice. Your gratitude compels you to bring glory to God by bearing much fruit. Spiritual multiplication is every disciple's earnest desire and responsibility (John 15:8).

Unfortunately, many believers hesitate to make this fundamental commitment to reproduction. Satan tells us that we are not good enough to make disciples. But do not be fooled. It is not your goodness, but the perfection of Christ in you that qualifies you to disciple others. It is not what you know but Who you know. If you have died to yourself, then Christ will reproduce His character through you.

God's Spirit used the same Peter who denied Christ three times to preach with power and boldness at Pentecost. When you willingly commit yourself to obeying your increasing knowledge of God's will, Christ transforms your weakness into strength. If you wait until you are perfect, you will never be a discipler. But when you step out in faith, God will build His kingdom through you.

Now let me add a word of caution. Discipling requires a constant commitment to self-death. Paul says, "For we who live are constantly being delivered over to death for Jesus' sake, that the life of Jesus also may be manifested in our mortal flesh" (2 Corinthians 4:11). John adds, ". . . we ought to lay down our lives for our brothers" (1 John 3:16 NIV).

Discipling is hard work. Paul "labored" to present every man complete in Christ (Colossians 1:28,29). The discipler makes a commitment to invest his *life* in his student: ". . . we were well-pleased to impart to you not only the gospel of God but also our own lives . . ." (1 Thessalonians 2:8). Spiritual parenting demands many hours each week for years. It calls for the expenditure of emotional energy. Paul asks, "Who is weak without my being weak? Who is led into sin without my intense concern?" (2 Corinthians 11:29). Pour-

ing your life into another person is a consuming investment.
Do not make a commitment before God to a discipling relationship until you count the cost.

When our ministry began, the need in the ghetto was so
overwhelming that virtually anyone who was willing to join
us was accepted on our staff. Many left after several months
"feeling" God was leading them elsewhere. But since we
minister primarily to the unchurched and since our staff
members work at full capacity, there was seldom anyone to
care for the spiritual children of the departing workers. All
too often I tried to explain to new believers that as soon as
another missionary came, we would resume the personal
attention their teacher had given them. But no matter what I
said, these babes in Christ seemed to hear, "You don't care
anymore. God doesn't love me anymore."

Too weak in the Lord to cope with a broken relationship,
these new believers fell by the wayside. Some threatened
suicide. Others reverted to stealing, drugs or prostitution.
Some died. Each had seen his teacher as a reflection of God,
and when he was abandoned, concluded that God Himself
was unfaithful. In an unstable culture like the ghetto, nothing could be worse than desertion.

God convicted us of this spiritual child-abandonment. A
God of excellence never wills for His work to be left unfin-
ished. We recognized that we needed to care for these new
believers until they were mature enough to feed themselves
spiritually and were incorporated into a healthy, functioning body. This is God's standard. Christ's work was not finished until His men were trained.

Realizing the gravity of our responsibility and knowing
the heart of God, we decided that each incoming staff member must make a commitment to God to minister with us at
least until he disciples someone to take over the ministry he
begins. There is no set time period. It might take five or ten
years, or even a lifetime. Such an open-ended commitment

seems unreasonable unless you are a dead man—living on borrowed time.

Since the cost of entering our discipling ministry is high, each potential staff member must carefully consider the implications. Ecclesiastes 5:4,5 (NIV) warns: "When you make a vow to God, do not delay in fulfilling it. He has no pleasure in fools; fulfill your vow. It is better not to vow than to make a vow and not fulfill it." If the applicant has any doubt, we suggest that he wait until God confirms his commitment to stick with it for the duration of the discipling process.

Recently a woman made this commitment to God in my presence and started to minister with us. Unfortunately a year later she changed her mind. She explained that God had led her to break her commitment in order to get married. I understood her desire to marry, but I knew that God was not the author of confusion (1 Corinthians 14:33). He does not "lie or change His mind . . ." (1 Samuel 15:29). A dead man knows that a commitment to God takes precedence over any subsequent opportunity. God would not call someone to lead people to Christ and then direct him to abandon these spiritual babes.

Intrinsic to spiritual parenting is an implied commitment to bring new believers to maturity. My heart grieves when Christian groups come to the ghetto, draw crowds through music, drama or token charity, and stimulate mass conversions—only to leave and have the audacity to expect that somehow these deserted converts will survive. I hurt when others invade urban America to practice their evangelistic skills in order to gain experience. They barrage entire communities with the spoken gospel, record numerous decisions and then retreat to the safety of their training camp to discuss their experiences. In one such blitz, their abandoned fruit was followed up by the Jehovah's Witnesses. Such "shotgun evangelism" displays contempt for the spiritual nurture which is the foremost concern of the New Testament epistles. To excite someone to become a believer without equipping him to lead the Christian life is cruel irresponsibility.

God will hold you accountable for the nurture of new believers over whom He has made *you* an overseer (Acts 20:28). You must focus all your energy on leading your disciples to reproduction.

Make a commitment in faith right now to obey Christ's command to make reproducing disciples. Then begin with one person. Christ's Church will be built through discipleship. Your personal investment will result in believers who are totally committed to serving God. And the explosive nature of spiritual multiplication makes fulfilling the Great Commission feasible. You were created to reproduce.

Discipler's Checklist—*Created to Reproduce*
☐ Spiritual multiplication is my earnest desire.
☐ I have a constant commitment to self-death.
☐ I am committed to bring new believers to maturity.
☐ I believe God will hold me accountable for the new believers over whom He has made me an overseer.

9
Choosing a
Disciple

Sandlot baseball was the rage in my neighborhood when I was a youngster. Every Saturday afternoon eight of us would split into teams and play until it was too dark to see. The success of my weekend was often determined by the quality of my teammates. Choosing the right players almost always led to victory.

The selection of the person whom you will disciple is crucial. The following principles have evolved from personal experience and I believe them to be indispensable in choosing a disciple.

Set a High Standard

Jesus made fishers of men only out of those who were willing to follow Him (Matthew 4:19). He demanded that His disciples give up everything they had, even their own lives if necessary, to follow Him. They had to meet His standard.

Five characteristics will help you identify a potential disciple:

1. He Desires to Know God Intimately

His teachable spirit indicates his hunger for God and thirst for righteousness. He seeks "to know Christ and the power of his resurrection and the fellowship of sharing in his sufferings, becoming like him in his death . . ." (Philippians 3:10 NIV). His consistent obedience to God demonstrates his self-death (James 1:22–25). God has said, "Let not a wise man boast of his wisdom, and let not the mighty man boast of his might, let not a rich man boast of his riches; but let him who boasts boast of this, that he understands and knows Me . . ." (Jeremiah 9:23,24).

2. He Is Available

Whenever there is an opportunity, he is willing and eager to be with you. His availability demonstrates the priority he places on your relationship. We always make time for things we think are important. Christ's disciples left their jobs to be with Him. Their availability proved their commitment.

3. He Is Submissive

He realizes that God accepts nothing less than a broken spirit (Psalms 51:17). His vulnerability and transparent communication demonstrate his trust in God and you. His servanthood and love for you reflect his submission and respect for your maturity. If he ministers to *you*, he is probably your person. Paul highly regarded Onesiphorus because he often refreshed and unashamedly served Paul (2 Timothy 1:16–18).

4. He Is Faithful

He is consistent in his Christian commitment, his routine responsibilities and his love for God. "Now it is required that those who have been given a trust must prove faithful" (1 Corinthians 4:2 NIV). God's Spirit places such a high value on faithfulness that He inspired Paul to make it the pivotal ingredient in determining which men should be trained (2 Timothy 2:2).

5. He Seeks to Become a Discipler

He understands that a mature Christian must be committed to discipling others. He desires to grow in the Lord so he can bring glory to God by reproducing Christ in others.

These five criteria may seem too lofty. But the quality you receive is determined by the standard you demand. If you will accept mediocrity, that is what you will get. Each year our directors review the guidelines for acceping new staff. Invariably, when we stiffen the requirements, the quality of the candidates is greatly improved. Do not be afraid to set a high standard.

Pray Diligently

Jesus chose His disciples only after ". . . He spent the whole night in prayer to God" (Luke 6:12). The Father gave Jesus the insight to see the potential of impetuous Peter, who would be called "Cephas," the rock (John 1:42). Behind the cynical Nathanael, He saw the character of one "in whom [there] is no guile" (John 1:47). God's guidance in the choice of a disciple is mandatory. ". . . man looks at the outward appearance, but the Lord looks at the heart" (1 Samuel 16:7).

There is no way you can entice someone to die to himself and enter a discipling relationship. Jesus taught, "No one can come to Me, unless the Father who sent Me draws him . . ." (John 6:44). Only God can prepare a person to become a disciple and to reproduce a Christ-like character in others. God Himself said, ". . . Set apart for me Barnabas and Saul for the work to which I have called them" (Acts 13:2 NIV).

Even Christ's disciples were given to Him by God (John 17:6).

The selection of a disciple demands diligent prayer. Together with your spiritual leaders ask God to direct you to the person He wants you to disciple.

Select Carefully

Jesus demonstrated His commitment to quality selection by choosing only a few men out of multitudes (Luke 6:13). Some who wanted to be with Him were told that they could not (Luke 8:38,39). Those who were overconfident, had the wrong priorities or clung to old affections were excluded (Luke 9:57–62). By concentrating on a few individuals, Jesus resisted the temptation to spread Himself too thin.

When you think you have found a potential disciple, develop a pre-discipleship relationship with him before inviting him to be discipled. Pre-discipleship is training a potential disciple how he "ought to live in order to please God" (1 Thessalonians 4:1 NIV). This relationship has two advantages. It equips him to grow from spiritual infancy through childhood, and it allows you to assess the depth of his commitment.

Pre-discipleship Training

Early converts in Jerusalem were nurtured by "continually devoting themselves to the apostles' teaching and to fellowship, to the breaking of bread and to prayer" (Acts 2:42).

First, your potential disciple must be incorporated into a healthy, functioning body where he can learn how to be like Christ by watching others and where he can experience the fellowship, love and accountability that he needs.

Further, you must encourage him to build a solid foundation for his Christian life. He needs to let his "roots grow

down into [Christ] and draw up nourishment from him . . ."
(Colossians 2:7 LB). This means that he must be equipped to
feed himself spiritually through regular Bible study, Scripture memorization, meditation, prayer and worship.

You must work closely with him in each of these disciplines in order to ensure that they become a part of his life.
Tell him why he should study, memorize, meditate, pray and
worship. Teach him from the Bible how important these are
and underscore their value by sharing your experience.
Point out that practicing these disciplines is not legalism,
but faithfulness. *Show him how* by sharing one or two ways
that you do them. *Get him started* by doing them with him.
Keep him at it. Your example will encourage him to be faithful. Regularly share principles you have learned and are applying. Be available to answer his questions. Hold him accountable for assignments and practical, daily applications.

When your student is faithfully involved in each of these
Christian fundamentals without your prodding, your pre-
discipleship relationship has been successful.

Close Observation

Pre-discipleship allows you to become better acquainted
with a potential disciple. You can monitor his motivation,
teachability and commitment to God and decide whether or
not to disciple him on the basis of his life, not merely on his
words.

It is essential that he incorporate the basics of Christianity
into his life and that you know him well before you initiate
a discipleship relationship. First Timothy 5:22 warns, "Do
not lay hands on anyone too hastily. . . ."

Take the Initiative

If God's Spirit confirms to you and those in authority
over you that you should enter a discipling relationship,
you must take the initiative. In God's compassion for unre-

pentant humanity He became flesh and dwelt among us (John 1:14). God took the initiative. When Christ began His discipling ministry, He called each disciple personally (John 6:70).

Issue the Invitation

Explain to your potential disciple that after much prayer and through the counsel of your spiritual leaders, God has led you to invite him to make a commitment to discipleship. Point out how his eagerness to know God, his availability, submissive spirit, faithfulness and vision to make disciples indicate that God has prepared him to be equipped to teach others.

Emphasize that your relationship will require a great deal of time. You will meet together in a structured setting at least three hours a week. He will be held accountable for written assignments, memory verses and regular Bible study. This minimum time commitment must be agreed upon in advance. Then, as he matures, his involvement with you in ministry will gradually increase. He must see his spiritual growth as his top priority.

Share how a one-on-one relationship with a mature Christian will provide quality training and meet his individual needs. Since you will progress at a pace that is sensitive to his spiritual development, he will acquire a thorough understanding of the Christian life-style.

Explain the Relationship

The purpose of a discipling relationship is to equip one who has died to himself to reproduce a Christ-like character in others. Explain to your potential disciple that without commitment and submission, yours is not a discipling relationship.

Commitment.   Tell him why you must be *committed to one another*. Explain that without a prior mutual commitment, you are likely to give up at the first sign of struggle or become discouraged by an indication of weakness. Consequently, you covenant together before God to grow into the fullness of His Son no matter what the cost. Commitment means no turning back, no boundaries, no reservations, no limits.

In 1975 I was flying from St. Louis to Los Angeles when the pilot announced a "serious threat" that a bomb was on board our flight. We made an emergency landing and were told to evacuate immediately. When we shoved the door open, a thin slide automatically ejected from the plane and started to inflate. It shot straight out, parallel to the ground. I hesitated for a moment, afraid to jump, but more afraid not to.

Before the slide even hit the ground, I hurled my body onto this tenuous exit. Words cannot describe my terror! But from the instant I jumped, I was bound by my decision.

Since God demands unwavering faithfulness, the discipleship commitment is as binding as that leap from the plane. Affirm to your potential disciple that once you make this commitment to each other, you are both bound to it. Assure him that your commitment will remain firm even when he stumbles. Explain that he must be committed to watching, listening, following and responding to your direction in order to come of age in Christ. Your unreserved commitment to each other is the foundation of your relationship.

Submission. Tell your potential disciple why he must submit to you as the one in whom God has invested authority to train him for reproduction. His submission is crucial because without it you cannot exercise authority over him. Christ called His disciples, but before He could begin training them, they had to follow Him.

Be sure your relationship is clearly defined and that your

potential disciple understands your respective roles. He needs to know that you are the leader because of your commitment and character, not because of your education or skills. Your leaders should explain to him that your active submission to them qualifies you for leadership. This will launch your relationship on the proper course and help establish your authority.

Your potential disciple must make a commitment to joyful submission. Hebrews 13:17 says, "Obey your leaders, and submit to them; for they keep watch over your souls, as those who will give an account. Let them do this with joy and not with grief, for this would be unprofitable for you." How can a leader experience joy if his disciple does not gladly submit to him? Share with your prospective disciple that there is comfort in knowing that you are accountable to God to guide him in his Christian walk and watch over his well-being.

More than anything else, submission means trust. Recently a young man who had experienced a dramatic conversion from drugs and crime through our ministry had an opportunity to share his testimony on national television. I counseled him not to do it at that time. Circumstances prevented me from explaining to him right then the reasons for my counsel. I simply asked him to trust. What a joy it was to me when he instantly agreed, because of his commitment to submission. Later I was able to share with him the danger of pride and the importance of "living out" his new life before premature public exposure.

Explain to your potential disciple that his submission provides security in finding God's will because he has the opportunity to seek your counsel. Assure him that if you do not know the answer, you will ask your leaders and he will receive an authoritative response rather than just an opinion. ". . . in multitude of counsellors there is safety" (Proverbs 24:6 KJV).

Your potential disciple must *actively* submit to you. Active submission is the opposite of mere acquiescence or passive obedience; it is taking the initiative in areas that affect one's growth. A disciple must eagerly seek his leader's direction in order to be guided to maturity. He must choose to be transparent and vulnerable in areas that might otherwise remain hidden. Ephesians 4:15 says that we all must speak the truth in love so that we will grow in Christ.

A disciple is quick to share his sorrows and failures. James 5:16 teaches, "Therefore, confess your sins to one another . . . so that you may be healed. . . ." He does not attempt to protect himself by hiding who he is. You cannot bear his burdens unless he shares them (Galatians 6:2). Failure to communicate his struggles demonstrates that he either does not <u>sincerely</u> want to know God's standard or that he does not choose to live by it.

One friend was having a debilitating struggle with lust. The blatant promiscuity of the ghetto had rendered him totally defeated. He had broken so many promises to God to keep a pure heart and a clean mind that he felt like an habitual liar.

Satan fought hard to emphasize that confession would mean losing leadership responsibilities and being severely restricted in his activities. But he knew that to continue without confession, cleansing and victory would destroy his usefulness and lead to reproducing carnality in others. Finally, he realized that he could not win this battle alone.

He determined that he wanted nothing less than Christlikeness, no matter what the cost. His responsibilities were curtailed, his freedom was limited and his pride suffered a staggering blow. But through close accountability, regular encouragement and much prayer, God gave him victory. Today he is pure and is ministering successfully.

By revealing difficult areas, your potential disciple will perpetuate his own growth and demonstrate his trust in you. The more actively he submits, the better the quality of training he will receive. Active submission is vital to his spiritual health. A dead man's only appropriate response to God and to his discipler is joyful and active submission.

Promise your potential disciple that on the basis of his submission, you will hold him accountable in all areas of his life. Paul held Archippus accountable: ". . . See to it that you complete the work you have received in the Lord" (Colossians 4:17 NIV). Every disciple experiences greater growth if he is responsible to another. Privately he can be praised, encouraged, challenged or admonished without stimulating pride or inflicting embarrassment.

The Christian life hinges on discipline, which will be developed in your disciple only as you hold him accountable. Paul encouraged the Thessalonians to follow his example of a disciplined life-style (2 Thessalonians 3:7). Although many of our new staff had been believers for years, they had not incorporated Bible study, Scripture memorization, meditation, prayer and worship into their daily lives. But when they committed themselves to a one-on-one relationship in which they were held accountable in these areas, a deeper devotion to God and a healthier Christian community resulted.

Communicate the Vision

Be sure your potential disciple understands that he is part of a process. First, his obedience to Jesus' command to follow Him required death to himself. Then, his pre-discipleship relationship equipped him to live the Christian life. You are now inviting him to become a functioning disciple—to be involved in evangelism and the pre-discipleship of another. As he matures in Christ, he will become a disciple-maker, one who actually invests his life in another disciple. Finally, when his disciple begins discipling others, he will become a leader of disciple-makers.

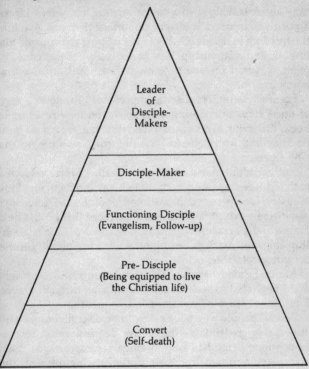

Your relationship is not meant merely to provide spiritual health in your disciple's personal life. No disciple is an end in himself, but a link in God's grand design to expand His Church through reproduction. He will be investing in others the rest of his life.

Let Him Decide

After thoroughly explaining the implications of disciple-ship, ask your potential disciple to take a week or two to pray about making such a commitment. Do not try to force a positive response. It is very important that you give him the freedom to decide. Only the Holy Spirit calls people to a discipleship relationship. If he is not ready for this commitment, it is best for you to know before you start investing hours in him.

I cannot overemphasize the importance of following each of these steps in choosing a disciple. You may be eager to begin discipling. This is commendable, but eagerness must be tempered with patience—waiting for God's timing and God's person.

Sadly, I admit that at one time or another I have neglected each of these steps, and every time it has short-circuited my ministry. One person demonstrated all of the characteristics of a disciple except faithfulness. Convinced that I could help him with that, I compromised God's standard. Our relationship lingered for eighteen months until his unfaithfulness became intolerable.

Another time I was so certain that a man's heart was right that I neglected to seek God's confirmation through prayer. This "ideal disciple" was gone in two months.

Several people who have asked to be discipled came with impeccable credentials—impressive degrees, lavish recommendations. I used to be too embarrassed to insist upon first watching them live their Christian commitment. But our relationship inevitably turned out to be pre-discipleship, nurturing immature believers in the Christian basics. The danger in this is that the student presumes he is being discipled and is therefore ready to disciple others. This prolongs his death-to-self and reinforces a misconception that his value lies in skills, not character. If you are in a pre-discipleship relationship, call it that, even if you are moving toward discipleship.

One time I initiated a discipleship relationship without defining what would be expected. The individual assured me that he knew what was involved, but he was never submissive. He didn't want to be discipled; he wanted fellowship without responsibility.

I pray that you will learn from my mistakes. If you follow these steps in choosing a disciple, the probability of quality reproduction will be high and the joy that you experience will be immeasurable.

Discipler's Checklist—*Choosing a Disciple*
- ☐ I have set a high standard for my disciple.
    - ☐ He desires to know God intimately.
    - ☐ He is available.
    - ☐ He is submissive.
    - ☐ He is faithful.
    - ☐ He seeks to become a discipler.
- ☐ I have prayed diligently.
- ☐ I have selected carefully.
- ☐ I have taken the initiative.
    - ☐ I have issued the invitation.
    - ☐ I have explained the relationship.
    - ☐ I have communicated the vision.
    - ☐ I have allowed him to decide.

10
Discipleship Is Relational

Discipleship is a life-on-life encounter. It is not merely a series of meetings or a set course of study. It is essentially relational—an investment of all that you are in another person. Your success in reproducing the fullness of life you have in Christ in your disciple will rise or fall according to the strength of your relationship.

Let me suggest eight qualities that will help you develop a healthy relationship with your disciple.

Warmth

Warmth is an attitude of love and gentleness conveyed through a blend of verbal and nonverbal communication.

Your *love* for one another is the most significant indicator of your love for Christ. First Peter 1:22 encourages Christians to love each other warmly with all their hearts. Unselfishness, servanthood and commitment constitute love and distinguish your submission-authority relationship from partnerships in the world.

Love seeks what is best for one's brother. It evidences itself in genuine concern. Paul said to Barnabas, ". . . Let us return and visit the brethren in every city in which we proclaimed the word of the Lord, and see how they are" (Acts 15:36). Your disciple is a friend, not a spiritual project. Listen to his hurts and comfort him in sorrow. Adopt his inter-

ests, concerns and joys as your own. Be sincerely interested
in people and events which affect him.

If you serve your disciple joyfully, he will know you love
him, and will respect you and seek your leadership. Paul
said, "And I will most gladly spend and be expended for
your souls . . ." (2 Corinthians 12:15). Sacrificial love will
inspire your disciple toward the mark of becoming "perfect
and complete, lacking in nothing" (James 1:4).

Your love for your disciple is grounded upon your commitment to him. It transcends emotional feelings. Many of
Christ's disciples abandoned Him and others denied that
they knew Him even while He was dying for them. But
Christ's commitment to them was unwavering: ". . . He
loved them to the end" (John 13:1). Paul's love made him
"willing to be forever damned" if it would save his people
(Romans 9:3 LB). Love motivates you to go the second mile
with your disciple, to extend yourself in order to encourage
and build him. It transforms a judgmental, abrupt or demanding spirit into forgiveness, forbearance and understanding.

Listen to the apostles' expressions of love to their spiritual children: "Having thus a fond affection for you . . ." (1
Thessalonians 2:8); "For I long to see you . . ." (Romans
1:11); ". . . I have you in my heart. . . . I long for you all with
the affection of Christ Jesus" (Philippians 1:7,8); "I have no
greater joy than this, to hear of my children walking in the
truth" (3 John 4).

Never be ashamed to tell your disciple that you love him.
Recently I phoned Norm Boswell in Newark, some 3,000
miles away, and simply said, "I love you." Norm was astounded and thrilled to find out that that was the only reason for my call. Susie surprised her disciple with a bouquet
of flowers. Mary unexpectedly picked up her disciple from
an appointment, just so she wouldn't have to walk home in
the rain. Affirm your love to your disciple.

However, explain that love also requires that your relationship not be exclusive. Death-to-self includes putting limits on cherished friendships for the sake of God's kingdom. Both of you must give and relate freely to others. Your relationship must be Christ centered, not self-centered.

Gentleness enhances your leadership. Paul was gentle "as a nursing mother tenderly cares for her own children" (1 Thessalonians 2:7). Your sensitivity to your disciple's feelings will stimulate his growth. He must have the assurance that your love for him will not be affected by his faults and humanness. Paul exhorts, "Now accept the one who is weak in faith . . ." (Romans 14:1).

One evening I was with a disciple who seemed unusually nervous. After a few minutes he tearfully confessed: "I lied to you." A month earlier he had told me that a man with whom I wanted an appointment was unavailable. Now he acknowledged that he had forgotten to call and had been afraid to tell me the truth.

I think he expected me to respond with hellfire and brimstone. I thought for a moment and then apologized for conveying such a demanding spirit that he had been afraid to admit his error. I assured him that our relationship was more important than any engagement and that my love for him was not affected by what he did or failed to do. He later shared that my acceptance of him that evening was the most significant factor in his believing that God could use him to make disciples.

If you speak of Christ's unconditional love and then show disgust when your disciple admits sin, your actions deny your words. Your life should communicate, "I love you. I'm on your side."

Gentleness requires tact, that keen perception of the correct thing to say or do without offending another. It allows you to remain true to your principles without triggering your disciple's defense mechanisms. Proverbs 15:23 (LB) observes, ". . . how wonderful it is to be able to say the right thing at the right time!"

Tact requires godly wisdom. James 3:17 teaches, "But the wisdom from above is first pure, then peaceable, gentle, reasonable, full of mercy and good fruits, unwavering, without hypocrisy."

A few years ago one of our staff members was transferred to another city. Upon her arrival she immediately pointed out many of the faults of that city's ministry and suggested how it could become more effective and efficient. The staff in the new city responded defensively, rejecting carte blanche everything she said.

Even though this young lady had the practical knowledge and experience that could have greatly benefited her new ministry, she lacked the skill of tact. She should have postponed threatening questions about their lives and work until they knew that she loved them. A barrage of questions is often interpreted as interrogation. People become defensive when others shoot holes in everything they are doing or suggest vast changes too quickly.

"The Lord is compassionate and gracious, Slow to anger and abounding in lovingkindness" (Psalms 103:8). Your Christ-like warmth guards the validity of the gospel. It stimulates the respect and openness of your disciple.

Loyalty

Loyalty is a consistent commitment to another person. It means standing by his side through thick or thin. Few things solidify a relationship like weathering a crisis together. "If you love someone you will be loyal to him no matter what the cost. You will always believe in him, always expect the best of him, and always stand your ground in defending him" (1 Corinthians 13:7 LB).

Your disciple must never question your loyalty. If he fails you, never express a lack of faith in him or hint that you want to abandon the relationship. Share your disappointments only with your leaders who can help you build him. Ephesians 4:29 instructs, "Let no unwholesome word proceed from your mouth, but only such a word as is good for edification according to the need of the moment. . . ."

There have been times when I have sincerely believed in and defended people to the hilt and later discovered that I was wrong. But I have never regretted being loyal. A dead man does not feel used or abused. He has nothing to lose by being loyal to his disciples.

Fairness

Fairness demands that you be unbiased. "For there is no partiality with God" (Romans 2:11), nor should there be with His people (James 2:1). Your disciple must know that you are fair.

I have the privilege of investing in nine people who direct our inner-city ministries across America. They have diverse backgrounds, varied intellectual capacities, unique personalities and different potentials.

I diligently attempt to accept each director for who he is and to develop his special talents and skills. I asked God to help me overcome any personality preferences which might hinder my usability and to protect me from motivating one disciple by comparing his growth to another's. The only uniform standard toward which we all strive is a Christ-like character.

It is unfair to demand or even hope for equality in Bible understanding, Scripture retention or ministry performance. Each person is God's own inimitable creation and must be treated accordingly.

If you try to lead your disciple with an inflexible, predetermined plan, it will be disastrous. If you try to make him fit into a certain desired mold you will be disappointed. Fairness demands that you respect his uniqueness and enjoy the variety in Christ's body.

If your disciple accuses another member in the body of a wrong, demonstrate that you are loyal and fair to each person. Do not agree or disagree until you have talked to both of them, preferably together. "... A quick retort can ruin everything" (Proverbs 13:3 LB). Listen to each point of view. Pray. Then seek the answer in God's Word and through your leaders. Help your disciple refocus on his purpose and objectives. Train him to ask for and give forgiveness. Together reaffirm your commitment to unity in the body to the glory of God. If your disciple knows that this is your policy, he will obey Zechariah 8:16 (LB): "... Tell the truth. Be fair. Live at peace with everyone."

Maturity

Maturity is a steady, faithful walk with God. Jesus claimed, "... I always do the things that are pleasing to Him" (John 8:29). Paul said, "You are witness, and so is God, how devoutly and uprightly and blamelessly we behaved toward you believers" (1 Thessalonians 2:10).

Since you seek to produce a wholeness in every area of your disciple's life, you must be consistently mature. He will learn servanthood, sensitivity and the correct attitude toward responsibility through your example. He will copy your conduct and respect your maturity.

The reverse is also true. Your disciple will monitor whether or not you live what you teach. He will watch you even when you are unaware of it. A sarcastic comment, a questionable joke, a lack of trust in your leaders or jealousy will be observed and reproduced.

Maturity never hinders the formation of a discipling relationship. When Marge was new to our staff, she was so anxious to develop close friendships with some teenagers that she did virtually everything they did. Her zeal was commendable and she became well liked by the girls. But over a period of months, we noticed that whenever any of the teens had a serious problem or wanted guidance for an important decision, they talked to our women's director instead of Marge. Marge had become just "one of the girls" and did not have their respect. Immaturity is too high a price to pay for acceptance.

Availability

Your disciple is your top priority in the body, unless you are married. If you are married, he is second only to your family. Even though Paul found an open door to preach the gospel in Troas, he left in order to find Titus (2 Corinthians 2:12,13). Titus was more important to Paul than the whole city of Troas. You must have a dogged determination to keep your disciple as your priority.

You and your disciple need maximum access to each other in order to have a quality relationship. You may need more than three hours of formal weekly meetings if you are having difficulty getting to know each other or if your disciple is insecure. While one meeting must be reserved for training, Bible study and accountability, additional times may be designed for fellowship, sharing and doing things together.

Be available to invest in and challenge your disciple even if his many questions or strong desire to learn demand a great deal of time. Do not stifle his fervor. Be particularly sensitive during times of adjustment or crisis. If he struggles with addictions such as impure thoughts or "doing" instead of "being," help him day and night.

When you obeyed Christ's command to follow Him, you relinquished your right to determine your own schedule. ". . . you are not your own. For you have been bought with a price . . ." (1 Corinthians 6:19,20). All of your time became God's time to be used in any way that best honors Him.

If you are too busy for your disciple when he needs you,

you are too busy. One disciple whom I love dearly phoned me at two in the morning and in a broken voice simply asked if we could meet immediately.

Without hesitation I rushed to the appointed place and spent several hours in prayer and counsel. It was the wisest investment I have ever made in terms of strengthening our love and commitment. He knew that I viewed him as a priority and that when his world was collapsing, I was there to help put the pieces back together. Moments like this record the principles governing a healthy relationship in indelible ink on the life of your disciple.

On a recent trip to Wichita my schedule was packed with staff training, public speaking and private meetings. As our director, Al Ewert, and I drove from appointment to appointment, we discussed his long list of ministry questions.

My final meeting went longer than expected, causing me to miss my flight. Since the next plane did not leave for four hours, I wearily suggested that we get a cup of coffee.

Once we sat down I shared some of the pressures, deadlines and emergencies with which I was dealing. Al's encouragement was like a cool breeze on a blistering summer day. Before long I was reflecting on my dreams and goals—how I believed God was about to do mightier things than either of us expected. Al affirmed my vision and added several inspiring thoughts God had given him.

The time passed quickly. As I boarded the plane I could hardly believe how refreshed I felt. Several days later, Al told me on the phone that for him our time in the coffee shop had been the highlight of my stay in Wichita—and it had certainly been mine.

Do not waste valuable time by taking long drives by yourself or by sitting alone in an airport. *Invite your disciple to be with you.* These are precious opportunities to teach, fellowship and be a consistent influence. Jesus "tried to avoid all publicity in order to spend more time with his disciples, teaching them . . ." (Mark 9:30 LB). He was never too busy, never too tired to meet their needs.

Patience

Patience means being slow to anger. It is faith in action, not passivity. Patience compels you to extend grace toward your disciple without compromising God's standard. It prevents bitterness. Patience is a trademark of a disciple-maker.

Jesus began with unqualified men who needed to be prompted and encouraged each step of the way. It took a long time for His disciples to develop godly characters, but the Lord kept working with His men until they became like Him. He never gave up on them. He endured the brashness of James and John, the fickleness of Peter and the doubting of Thomas. That was patience.

God promises to give His children this same Christ-like patience (Romans 15:5). Disciple-makers must wait for God's timing and direction. Your disciple may be afraid of people, he may resist change or struggle with priorities. These obstacles can be overcome as he watches you and as the Holy Spirit works in his life. But you must be patient.

It takes a long time to make disciples. In the ghetto we may spend six months building a friendship with a person and then an additional six months before he makes a commitment to Christ. We may spend a year nurturing this new believer and then another three years discipling him to the point of reproduction. Nevertheless, five years of investment in one person is well worth the effort if he becomes a reproducing disciple.

The first time we met Virgil was shortly after he broke our windows and robbed our women's staff home in Los

Angeles. That was seven years ago. Today he is being trained to disciple others. Not one of our staff regrets this time investment.

In the ghetto most of us have prayed for and invested time in people who later rejected Christ. But we do not become discouraged. We keep on. "God Himself has given us this wonderful work and so we never give up. We are perplexed because we don't know why things happen as they do, but we don't give up and quit. We get knocked down, but we get up again and keep going" (2 Corinthians 4:1,8,9 LB).

Neither skepticism nor opposition should deter your commitment to invest in your disciple. When your patience is tested, affirm your faith in God's sovereignty by claiming Philippians 1:6: "For I am confident of this very thing, that He who began a good work in you will perfect it until the day of Christ Jesus."

Honesty

The basis for every healthy relationship is honest communication. This is built on your commitment to one another and the knowledge that transparency is for your own good. Ephesians 4:25 instructs us to lay aside falsehood and speak the truth. Your relationship will not grow unless both you and your disciple communicate openly. You must be aware of each other's needs and feelings. Do not expect your partner to be perfect, just honest and genuine.

I know of nothing that better fosters honesty than the intimacy of a discipleship relationship. Many believers are ashamed to share their struggles or anxieties, afraid that their most private burdens will be transformed into gossip. But your disciple knows you will guard his reputation. He can confidently talk with you about anything because he is secure in your love for him. ". . . perfect love casts out fear . . ." (1 John 4:18) so that we may "walk in the light . . ." (1

John 1:7). Your disciple must communicate anything that may affect him, the body or his ministry even when he does not feel like it.

Encourage honesty in your student by communicating yourself, by listening and by being open to criticism.

Communicate yourself. If you honestly share your struggles, hurts and disappointments, as well as your victories, dreams and accomplishments, your disciple will soon share his own. If you make a mistake, admit it, but always do this with a view toward building the kingdom and strengthening his character. Your openness will communicate, "I'm teachable and I trust you." It will inspire honest communication.

Several years ago Joan had a close friendship with a fine man. People assumed they would get married, but God revealed to them that they should not pursue the relationship. Joan's teenage Bible students were anxious to know why the relationship ended and how she felt. Even though it was painful, Joan rehearsed the principles God had taught them and confided her struggles—the hurt, the loneliness and even the fear of remaining single. Her girls were amazed by her openness. Joan trusted them to minister to her!

Joan's transparency during that crisis powerfully communicated her love for her girls. This freed them to share their struggles. By watching God work in Joan's life, they became confident in His power to meet their needs. Today, four of them are functioning disciples.

Do not lose your disciple's respect, however, by destructive sharing. Some immature Christians stumble or justify their sins because of their leader's failures. Others become insecure or lose confidence in their leader if he appears weak. If you have any doubt about sharing something, check with your leaders first.

It is unfair to expect your disciple to carry too many of

your deep concerns. Overcommunication, even if it is pure and truthful, can cause him to become proud or discouraged. Jesus told His disciples, "I have many more things to say to you, but you cannot bear them now" (John 16:12). Be sensitive to God's guidance regarding what and how much to share.

Listen. When your disciple talks to you, concentrate on what he has to say. Your undivided attention proves that you care. If you are preoccupied with how you will respond instead of listening intently to his thoughts, you will communicate disinterest. Indicate that you understand by both nonverbal and verbal affirmation. Ask probing questions that will encourage his openness. But do not interrupt him. "A wise man holds his tongue . . ." (Proverbs 10:14 LB).

Be open to constructive criticism. Demonstrate trust in your disciple by encouraging constructive criticism. Listen carefully when your disciple shares criticism. Consider his ideas. He is in a unique position to mirror your strengths and weaknesses and enlighten you about how your personality projects things you may not intend. Apologize for your mistakes and then affirm your commitment to work at correcting them. Periodically, consult your disciple to see if the weakness he brought to your attention is improving. Thank him for his interest. "It is a badge of honor to accept valid criticism" (Proverbs 25:12 LB).

Mary Thiessen, our Los Angeles women's director, is a gifted teacher. She works hard to pass on her skills to her disciples by critiquing their teaching. But recently one of Mary's disciples approached her with a problem: "Your correction makes me so nervous that I can't teach well when you're around." Mary graciously accepted this constructive criticism and now tempers her suggestions for improvement with honest praise for her disciple's accomplishments.

Mary's openness strengthened their relationship.

The one qualification to giving or receiving criticism is that it must be responsible and sincere, not destructive. Do not play games with each other. Do not joke or try to rid yourself of a frustration at the expense of the other. Jesus warned that "... every careless word that men shall speak, they shall render account for it in the day of judgment" (Matthew 12:36).

If the criticism is emotionally charged, set a time to meet later so you can both think through the situation. James 1:19 teaches, "... But let every one be quick to hear, slow to speak and slow to anger."

If conflicts in your relationship result from personal opinion or preferences, listen and discuss. Be considerate and flexible. First Peter 4:8 says, "Above all, keep fervent in your love for one another, because love covers a multitude of sins." You can be united even while you are working out differences if you are both seeking God's will. Never give up under the guise of "personality clash" as though such a problem were insurmountable. Difficult relationships purify and sharpen us (Proverbs 27:17).

When your disciple knows he has the freedom to correct you, he will listen and act upon your correction. Proverbs 15:31 promises, "He whose ear listens to the life-giving reproof Will dwell among the wise."

Motivation

Motivation is that impelling desire which moves us toward our purpose. Motivation spurs your disciple on to be God's person and to minister effectively and joyfully.

When I was asked to lead a session on discipleship at a recent staff retreat I hesitated for fear of boring my coworkers. I live, breathe and eat discipleship and assumed that all of our staff was equally self-motivated.

But when I challenged them, I was astounded by the re-

sponse. Person after person told me how he had needed that
fresh motivation. Some had been so buried in teaching
Bible classes, responding to emergencies and conducting a
myriad of other ministry activities that they had lost sight of
their goal. They needed help in picturing how their seemingly mundane responsibilities were crucial to discipleship.
Even full-time missionaries can have their vision blurred by
the tyranny of the routine. We all need frequent motivation
to press on toward the mark.

Let me suggest four ways to motivate your disciple.

1. Direction.   You must have direction in your life in
order to lead your disciple. Paul declared, "However, I consider my life worth nothing to me, if only I may finish the
race and complete the task the Lord Jesus has given me . . ."
(Acts 20:24 NIV). Christ's disciples watched Him set out for
Jerusalem *with determination* to die for the sins of man (Luke
9:51). If you are growing in your knowledge of the Word
and consistently applying it in daily decision making, your
disciple will be motivated to do the same.

2. Vision.   Regularly bolster your disciple's vision for
discipleship. Christ was a discipler. And people were His
program. Your disciple must be convinced that "the one
who says he abides in [Christ] ought himself to walk in the
same manner as He walked" (1 John 2:6). Show your disciple that Paul's training of the Thessalonians resulted in their
effective ministry not only in Macedonia and Achaia, but in
every place that they went (1 Thessalonians 1:7,8). Remind
your disciple that his costly investment of time and energy
in others will also produce abundant and lasting fruit.

No wise man ignores the explosive potential of one person. Through Adam we all were born in sin, but through
Christ we have the potential for new life (1 Corinthians
15:22). Help your disciple keep his eye on the target of

making disciples. "Where there is no vision, the people perish . . ." (Proverbs 29:18 KJV).

3. Confidence. A confident person is stable, unwavering under pressure, because he rests in an unchanging and consistent God. Help your disciple find his confidence in Christ. When the apostles were unable to heal the epileptic boy, their confidence in the flesh was shattered and they turned to Christ (Mark 9). Do not protect your disciple from circumstances in which he can see his inadequacy. Give him responsibilities that will force him to trust God. His confidence will grow as he watches God honor his faith. If your disciple is aware of the presence and work of the living Christ in his life, Christian maturity and ministry are unavoidable.

The same Jesus who healed the sick, walked on water, raised the dead and then conquered death promised that those who believe in Him shall do even greater works (John 14:12). No person can be more confident than one who walks with Jesus.

4. Urgency. A disciple's ministry of reconciliation gains urgency when he recognizes that rejection of God's gift results in eternal damnation. Jesus warns, "We must work the works of Him who sent Me, as long as it is day; night is coming, when no man can work" (John 9:4). Compassion for others and the knowledge of Christ's imminent return demand urgency.

Yet, if the sense of urgency is too great, your disciple will become discouraged, feeling that there is so much to be done so quickly that his contribution would be insignificant. People function poorly under a constant siege of pressure.

Jesus preserved a delicate balance by imploring His disciples to act as if He would return at any moment—while di-

recting them to plan to build His Church for generations.
The urgency produced by His impending return prevented
laziness and procrastination among His followers, who then
proceeded to build His Church through discipleship. You
too must instill a well-balanced sense of urgency that motivates your disciple to act without frustrating him to inac-
tion.

A strong relationship is inseparable from successful discipling. It supplies you with the necessary understanding of
your disciple's spiritual health and provides a forum from
which you can direct him to reproduction. It gives him the
security to accept and the motivation to act upon your
input. And it is practical training for his eventual leading of
others. Christian discipleship is relational.

Discipler's Checklist—*Discipleship is Relational*
My relationship with my disciple is characterized by:
☐ Warmth—an attitude of love and gentleness.
☐ Loyalty—a consistent commitment.
☐ Fairness—being unbiased.
☐ Maturity—a steady, faithful walk with God.
☐ Availability—maximum access.
☐ Patience—faith in action.
☐ Honesty—open communication.
☐ Motivation—an impelling desire that moves us to-
         ward our purpose.

11

The Dynamics
of Discipleship

Your disciple's eagerness to know God, his availability, submission, faithfulness and vision indicate his readiness to be discipled. Your Christ-like character and the relationship you have with him qualify you to disciple him. However, without certain other elements he will never become reproductive. He will be like an engine without fuel or a windmill without a breeze—great potential but static and dormant.

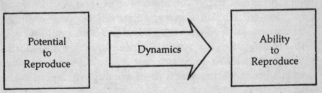

In order to transform your disciple's willingness to bear fruit into the ability to reproduce, his spiritual environment must include seven elements. If even one is missing, your disciple's training will be deficient. These are the dynamics of discipleship, the energizers. Once they become a natural part of your disciple, they will produce a godly character. When he understands them so well that he can pass them on to others, he is ready to be reproduced. You are responsible to impart these dynamics to him.

Even though discipling is a life-on-life encounter, you must set regular times to meet together each week. Let your personalities determine the structure of your meetings and let his needs dictate the content. However, do not expect these meetings alone to stimulate his growth. Real-life experiences and personal interaction continue to be paramount.

Worship

The primary purpose of your relationship is to honor and glorify God. Worship is that attitude of adoration which expresses your love, awe and respect for Almighty God. Your example will encourage your disciple to present his whole life to God as worship.

God has not prescribed a set form of worship for us to follow. Jesus taught that ". . . no one puts new wine into old wineskins; otherwise the wine will burst the skins, and the wine is lost, and the skins as well; but one puts new wine into fresh wineskins" (Mark 2:22). Since your relationship with God is new daily, you are free to express your love and adoration for Him in a manner that reflects your feelings.

If you are saddled with traditional methods your worship will become stale. But when you seek to honor and glorify God in all that you do, your heart and mind focus on Him, and His Spirit teaches you how to worship with spontaneity and freedom.

Worship with your disciple regularly. You can read, quote or sing Scripture. You can eat meals with other believers with gladness. You can pray, meditate, compose musical or poetic expressions of your joy, clap your hands, play an instrument or simply bow your head in humble adoration.

Katie and I were expecting only one child when Joshua

and Paul were born. Even though I praised God verbally for my sons, I suspect the greatest expression of my worship was a grin. I'm told it was solidly embedded on my face for days. In appreciation for who God is and what He has done for you, joy should exude from your life like fragrance from a flower.

God is much more concerned that you worship Him sincerely than He is about how you worship Him. There is no magic in simply saying "praise God." If your spirit and lifestyle are not in harmony with your words, "praise God" becomes idle talk or blasphemy, taking the Lord's name in vain. Don't fall into the pharisaical trap of obeying the letter of the law while making a mockery of its spirit.

When your worship is led by the Spirit, it is a response to God that glorifies Him (1 Corinthians 10:31), strengthens the body (1 Corinthians 14:3, 12) and builds you and your disciple (1 Corinthians 10:23).

Ministry

Minister to each other. Encourage one another with Scripture. Rejoice in your victories. Share your burdens and confess your sins. Then pray specifically about these concerns, claiming God's healing and forgiveness.

Praying for each other must become a regular part of your lives. Jesus beseeched the Father on behalf of His disciples, "I do not ask Thee to take them out of the world, but to keep them from the evil one. . . . Sanctify them in the truth . . ." (John 17:15,17). Paul told Timothy, ". . . I constantly remember you in my prayers night and day" (2 Timothy 1:3) and he pleaded with the Ephesians to "pray on my behalf . . ." (Ephesians 6:19).

The vitality of your relationship depends upon your prayers for one another. Pray for each other's protection (2 Corinthians 13:7) and growth (Colossians 1:9,10). Ask God for guidance as you counsel your disciple and seek to meet his needs. James encourages us, "But if any of you lacks wisdom, let him ask of God, who gives to all men generously and without reproach, and it will be given to him" (James 1:5).

This time of ministering to each other is crucial. When our work was young, I would often greet my men with a barrage of questions about the ministry. My exuberance to reach others and meet the needs of a hurting world overshadowed my concern for the spiritual welfare of my disciples. I just assumed that they were victorious in their personal lives.

Unfortunately, if they were struggling with a weakness or sin that had not been dealt with, our times together were unproductive. It's easy to succumb to "doing" before "being." The character and needs of my disciples are now a higher priority than their ministry. Your times together should build up and edify both of you.

Memorization

Scripture memorization is becoming a lost art in Christianity. Yet the Bible frequently urges believers to keep God's Word within them (Proverbs 7:1). Moses insisted that God's people keep His Word in their hearts (Deuteronomy 6:6). Scripture memory is our best defense against sin (Psalms 119:11). When Jesus was tempted by Satan, God's Spirit brought His Word to memory and provided immediate, sustaining power (Luke 4:4–12).

Scripture memorization is an invaluable ally in molding a Christ-like character. It is the basis for wise counsel and correction. One woman disciple was crippled by insecurity and immaturity that stemmed from rejection and mockery during childhood. With all her heart she wanted God to free her from this self-hatred, but inner peace and self-acceptance seemed completely out of reach. Then her discipler memorized Scripture with her about the attributes of God.

Week after week they reviewed these verses. Within a few months, God's Word produced in her a new depth of holiness, maturity and security.

Scripture memorization will engrave God's will on the heart of your disciple (Psalms 37:31). It facilitates worship and fellowship (Ephesians 5:19). Memorize one or two verses together each week and review others you have learned previously. Pray one of the memorized verses for each other every day during the week. You and your disciple must heed Colossians 3:16: "Let the Word of Christ richly dwell within you. . . ."

Meditation

Meditation is striving toward God-consciousness, a constant awareness of Him through reflection and devotion (Psalms 1:2). It is a natural consequence of your love for God's Word (Psalms 119:47). Meditation isolates you in the presence of God and produces the peace, trust and calm that can only be found in Him.

One night while I was in the Midwest, Mary Thiessen called me from Los Angeles. Some gang members had threatened to rape and kill her. I wanted to come home immediately to comfort her and to ensure her protection, but that was impossible. So I told her that through meditating on the word *Immanuel*, "God with us," I had often received peace. I encouraged Mary to do the same.

Mary relates, "I thought about *Immanuel* countless times during the next few days and finally experienced peace. And even now when we're in danger, meditating on *Immanuel* brings calm and confidence."

Reflection on the Word of God transformed Jeremiah's bitterness and loneliness into joy (Lamentations 3:18–23). We meditate on God's Word so that we "may be able to comprehend with all the saints what is the breadth and length and height and depth, and to know the love of Christ which surpasses knowledge . . ." (Ephesians 3:18,19).

Teach your disciple that dwelling on his fears and circumstances leads to worry and anxiety, while meditation focuses his mind on God, who is his strength (Psalms 46:1). Since we are so profoundly influenced by what we think, meditation will produce obedience (Psalms 119:15) and joy (Jeremiah 15:16).

Meditate on a verse that you have memorized. Let me suggest two ways that will help you to begin meditating with your disciple.

1. Ask some application questions about the verse:
   What does this verse tell me about God?
   What other truth does this verse teach?
   Is there a habit I should discontinue or a practice I should initiate?
2. Repeat aloud several times a verse you have memorized. Each time emphasize a different word or phrase. For example, in John 15:16:
   I chose you to go and bear fruit
   I *chose* you to go and bear fruit
   I chose *you* to go and bear fruit
   I chose you *to go* and bear fruit
   I chose you to go and *bear* fruit
   I chose you to go and bear *fruit*

Enjoy the truth and new insight that each emphasis brings to this verse. Share your thoughts with each other.

Teaching

Christ instructed His disciples to teach people "to observe *all* that I commanded you." Paul taught "the whole purpose of God" (Acts 20:27). He wrote, "And we proclaim Him, admonishing every man and teaching every man with all wisdom, that we may present every man complete in Christ" (Colossians 1:28).

Teach your disciple the Bible. After Jesus "opened their minds to understand the Scriptures" (Luke 24:45), He instructed His disciples to "feed My lambs" (John 21:15–17 KJV). What is more nourishing than the "living and active" Word of God (*see* Hebrews 4:12)? Here God reveals Himself and His will to man (Proverbs 2:1–5). Approach the Word with the same anticipation as the Psalmist: "Open my eyes, that I may behold Wonderful things from Thy law" (Psalms 119:18).

Your lessons must be accurate and practical. Systematically teach your disciple scriptural principles and doctrine that will help him mature in Christ. He must possess a *working* knowledge of Scripture in order to consistently apply biblical truth.

Jesus was a superb communicator. He taught with authority (Matthew 7:29) and people "enjoyed listening to Him" (Mark 12:37). Some exclaimed, "... Were not our hearts burning within us while He was speaking to us ... while He was explaining the Scriptures to us?" (Luke 24:32).

In order to stimulate your disciple's learning, you must be well prepared and should observe the following teaching principles.

Be creative. Jesus skillfully combined formal messages with informal chats. He both lectured and discussed, using real-life examples such as coins, lilies, seeds and soil to illustrate deep truths. How could the disciples ever forget Christ's lesson on power and faith when He cursed the fig tree (Matthew 21:19)?

Variety helps to maintain interest. Alternate between book and topical studies. Periodically change the place where you meet. Occasionally let your disciple teach you. This will help him understand the principles more thoroughly and will equip him to teach others. It will also allow you to evaluate his comprehension of the material.

Involve your disciple as you study. He will learn better how to study by studying with you than by listening to a lecture or trying to study on his own. Draw out biblical principles and become involved in practical applications together. He needs to see that you are just as hungry for the things you are teaching as you expect him to be.

Repeat important lessons or principles. Paul said, ". . . To write the same things again is no trouble to me, and it is a safeguard for you" (Philippians 3:1). Peter declared, "Therefore, I shall always be ready to remind you of these things, even though you already know them . . . " (2 Peter 1:12).

Be flexible. You will need to strike a delicate balance between meeting your disciple's immediate needs and having a fixed strategy for teaching. This can frequently be done by applying principles from that day's lesson to your disciple's needs.

Teach your disciple how to think.   When your disciple became a new creation in Christ, God renewed his mind (1 Corinthians 2:12). Now God requires that he *use* his regenerated faculties. Paul exhorts, "And do not be conformed to this world, but be transformed by the renewing of your mind, that you may prove what the will of God is . . ." (Romans 12:2).

Christ taught His disciples how to think by forcing them to arrive at their own deductions. He asked provocative questions that stimulated self-discovery. He would often respond to their questions with other questions. His teaching in parables encouraged them to ponder the meaning of His words.

Teach your disciple how to think by encouraging him to employ discovery methods of Bible study. Direct him to a biblical passage and let him ferret out the truths contained in it. Pose questions or give suggestions that point the way. Reword his questions and ask him what he thinks. Never answer a question that he has not tried to answer. He will learn biblical principles better if he finds them himself than if he receives a pat answer or a proven formula from you.

For example, if Fred Stoesz, our Los Angeles men's director, asked me whether Thuan or Charles should lead a one-on-one relationship with a new staff member, I would direct him to study 1 Timothy 3. Then I would ask him several questions: Who is best equipped to train this man? Who has the most available time? Are there other people who might lead the new staff member better? Who do you think is the best choice? Why? Fred usually arrives at the correct solution himself.

Encourage your disciple to write you as often as he desires. Written communication promotes accuracy and clarity by enabling him to think through his questions and needs. Frequently, he will pinpoint his area of concern or discover the answers himself while writing.

Teach your disciple how to make decisions. Jesus insisted that His disciples' decisions be based on the will of God. When Christ's disciples had received God's will through His words (John 14:24), they were equipped to make decisions (John 17:8).

Since a disciple's decision-making process is based on the will and Word of God it differs substantially from the self-centered, worldly approach. Teach your disciple that to avoid incorrect decisions that will adversely affect the cause of Christ he must answer four questions:

1. *What are the alternatives?* Your disciple must evaluate objectively all of the possible options by talking with those who know the facts and with those who will be affected by the decision. He needs adequate data to decide wisely. Proverbs 15:28 counsels: "The heart of the righteous ponders how to answer. . . ." Snap de-

cisions made under pressure are generally no more than guesses.

2. *What biblical principles apply?* Since your disciple is committed to doing the will of God, no decision should contradict a biblical principle. Mature thinking based on God's Word leads to confident decision-making and Christ-exalting actions.

3. *What are the implications?* Your disciple must examine the possible far-reaching effects of the decision. A little forethought can avoid many mistakes and sorrows.

4. *What is the counsel of my leaders?* Once your disciple has thought out the alternatives, principles and implications, he should present these to you. Pray and study God's Word together, seeking His direction. Your disciple must be "diligent to preserve the unity of the Spirit in the bond of peace" (Ephesians 4:3). Since cooperation in the body preserves unity, the best decisions are reached when they are made together with those in authority over you. Seeking counsel will help him to avoid making decisions that appear building but may hurt others because he is unaware of vital factors. Each situation is different and demands specific prayer and guidance.

Let me illustrate how this works. Suppose that you are on our staff and have just finished an extremely exhausting ministry month. Your leaders have planned a retreat to refresh the staff. Then, just as you are about to leave, you receive a call informing you that the home of one of your Bible club families has burned down.

Your immediate reaction may be to miss the retreat so you can aid the family. But as a Christian, you must make this decision in light of what is most building for the kingdom and the body. Important decisions like this demand well-thought-out action, not merely an emotional response. Let's apply our four-step decision-making process to this situation:

1. *What are the alternatives?* (a) Miss the retreat and respond to the family; (b) Respond to the family and try to take a break later; (c) Ignore, postpone or delegate the responsibility to meet the club family's need.

2. *What biblical principles apply?* (a) Psalms 46:1 teaches that a Christian's strength is found in God; (b) Mark 6:31 acknowledges that Christians need to be refreshed; (c) James 2:15,16 instructs Christians to be available to meet their neighbors' needs.

3. *What are the implications?* (a) If you miss the retreat you may hinder your effectiveness by ignoring a deep need to focus on God and be refreshed; (b) If you try to take a break later, you may have to cancel many ministry activities already planned. This could hurt other relationships or negate your teaching on faithfulness; (c) If you ignore the club family's need, you could hurt your relationship with them and lose a great opportunity to demonstrate Christian love.

4. *What is the counsel of my leaders?* If my guidance were sought in a situation like this, in which there are two conflicting priorities, I would review the alternatives and then consider the implications of each course of action in light of our priorities: God first, the body second, the ministry third. How badly do you need a break now? Can you get away with some other staff members later without jeopardizing your ministry? Is there someone else who could just as effectively respond to this need and who might suffer less by missing the retreat at this time?

After considering these, and any other applicable questions, we would commit the decision to the Lord in prayer and believe that God's Spirit would reveal His perfect will and confirm it to us. Seeking counsel in decision making provides wisdom and unity.

When your disciple makes every decision in light of the welfare of the kingdom and the body, he not only respects the health of the entire community, but he can be confident that he will receive the best guidance for himself.

When Christ left this earth His disciples knew God's Word and understood how to think and make decisions. Be sure your disciple is taught these essential lessons.

Correct Weaknesses

One of the hardest things for me to do when I began ministering was to correct another person. I dreaded rejection and feared that I might be wrong. An old preacher changed my whole perspective. He told me, "You're just a mouthpiece. Don't give your opinions or suggestions. If you can't preface it with 'Thus saith the Lord,' don't say it. But if the Bible says it and you're scared to declare it, you don't love the person."

Inevitably, there will be areas of your disciple's life which will not yet be Christ-like. You are responsible to expose and deal with these weaknesses (Galatians 4:19). You will be tempted to rationalize, "He's had a hard life," or "That is just part of his personality." But you must love your disciple enough to become involved in correcting his weaknesses. The following process is suggested for this purpose.

Discern his weaknesses. Carefully observe your disciple and listen to what he says. He is your greatest source of information concerning his needs and spiritual welfare.

Ask him questions that will help him express how he is doing and what his needs are. Concentrate on his life, his time in the Word and his relationships with others.

Watch him relate to those in authority over him, to his family, to strangers, to the opposite sex and to his friends. Discern how others view your disciple. Listen to the comments made about him. Is he respected? Credible? Liked? Check his written assignments and memory work. Do all this in love, but with a careful eye toward areas of need.

Confront your disciple. Once you have discerned a weakness, discuss this with your disciple. Love him enough to confront him. God says, "Those whom I love I rebuke and discipline ..." (Revelation 3:19 NIV). If your disciple strays from God's will, be courageous enough to call him back to the correct path. Paul was "exhorting and encouraging and imploring each one ... as a father would his own children" (1 Thessalonians 2:11). If you respond weakly or are intimidated by your disciple's rebellion, his training will be deficient.

Your disciple will respond positively to your confrontation if it is firm but loving. Paul told Timothy that he should "correct, rebuke and encourage—with great patience and careful instruction" (2 Timothy 4:2 NIV). But he told Titus to "... speak to the Christians ... as sternly as necessary to make them strong in the faith" (Titus 1:13 LB).

Paul was gentle but direct when he challenged Timothy about his reticence (2 Timothy 1). Paul began by affirming his love for Timothy (vv. 1–4) and recalling details of their intimate relationship (vv. 5,6). Then, based on this expressed closeness, he boldly addressed Timothy's need: "For God has not given us a spirit of timidity, but of power and love and discipline. Therefore do not be ashamed of the testimony of our Lord, or of me His prisoner ..." (vv. 7,8).

Always base your confrontation on God's Word and the authority of Jesus Christ. Then you can be as bold and confident as Christ was when He confronted Peter: "... Get behind Me, Satan; for you are not setting your mind on God's interests, but man's" (Mark 8:33). Paul wrote, ". . . We request and exhort you in the Lord Jesus . . ." (1 Thessalonians 4:1).

Show your disciple the biblical principles which expose his sinful actions and habits. This will establish that God's Word, not your opinion or experience, is the basis for correcting him.

However, do not confront your disciple each time you meet with him. Some time ago I noticed this tendency in my life. Because of the widespread nature of our ministry, there were some staff members whom I seldom saw. When I did see them it was because they had a serious problem that demanded my personal attention. After a period of time a very natural thing happened. When they were told Keith wanted to see them, they felt guilty and anxious. This dread was similar to that of a Roman Christian being invited to the Colosseum rather than the anticipation of meeting with a concerned brother who loved him. No one wants a relationship that is built on confrontation.

Be sure to balance your confrontation with encouragement and support. Compliment your disciple for his growth and application of God's principles. Share how he ministers to you. He must have this affirmation.

Once you have confronted your disciple, study the Bible together to find the positive characteristic that needs to be developed in his life or encourage him to discover the standard for himself.

Pray together.   Only God can change a life (1 Corinthians 3:6). Paul urged his friends to "agonize" with him in prayer (Romans 15:30). Jesus promised, ". . . If two of you agree on earth about anything that they may ask, it shall be done for them by My Father . . ." (Matthew 18:19). Make a commitment in prayer to turn this weakness into a strength.

Develop a strategy. A strategy is a series of steps that will lead your disciple to the achievement of his goal. These steps must be specific, clearly defined and attainable. Let me suggest three vital elements that must be included in every strategy to eliminate weakness.

1. *Bible study.* Many do not study the Bible because it rebukes them. But change occurs through the "encouragement of the Scriptures . . ." (Romans 15:4). God richly blesses those who obey Him.

   George was a staff member who frequently turned his reports in late. His leader explained the inconvenience this caused, but George failed to correct this weakness until he studied about faithfulness in small things. That changed his attitude. Studying passages that speak directly to the problem must be included in the strategy.

2. *Positive models.* Your disciple will learn to follow Christ by watching you and other mature believers who can furnish positive models of the needed characteristic. Peter told the elders to be examples to the flock (1 Peter 5:1–3). Paul encouraged the Philippians to "Join with others in following my example, brothers, and take note of those who live according to the pattern we gave you" (Philippians 3:17 NIV). Your lives will demonstrate that it is possible for the disciple to obey God in the area of his weakness. He must be exposed to the needed trait. An example is a powerful agent of change.

3. *Practical application.* James 1:22 (RSV) exhorts us to ". . . be doers of the word, and not hearers only . . . ." Your disciple will grow through specific application. Involve him in activities that will help correct his weakness. For example, he will learn servanthood by cleaning up after a group meeting. He should not par-

ticipate in activities that are detrimental to his maturing in his area of weakness. Leading a Bible study may feed his pride and be counterproductive.

Your disciple must see this strategy as his, not one you have forced on him. Incorporate his ideas whenever possible. Affirm that you will support and encourage him in following this plan.

Hold him accountable. Even though this is a long process it is excellent time stewardship. If your disciple understands the principles and knows how to apply them, he will be effectively equipped to deal with future weaknesses in his life and in the lives of those whom he will lead. Equally important, this process will verify your love for him and reinforce his trust in you as one who seeks God's will in every decision you make. Since trust is the basis for submission, dealing with his weaknesses in this manner will help him joyfully submit to God's authority.

Develop His Strengths

In order to foster your disciple's growth and develop his God-given gifts, you are responsible to cultivate his strengths.

First, be sure that his apparent strengths are not a source of pride. If they are, deal with them as weaknesses. Then design a strategy to develop his areas of strength. This strategy must include Bible study, positive models and practical application as discussed above. It is ideal if you can assign a project that will correct a weakness and develop a strength simultaneously.

Ruth was weak in organizing, but strong in servanthood. So we gave her the responsibility of overseeing the meals for our Los Angeles staff. This included planning the menus, organizing the shopping and assigning the cooks. Her servanthood motivated others to willingly do their jobs.

This built her strength. And Ruth became a good organizer, correcting her weakness. In response to your prayer, God will give you discernment to see undeveloped strengths in your disciple.

Upon completion of any project, evaluate your disciple's effectiveness. Ask him what worked. Why did it work? What didn't work? Why not? How could you improve? What was accomplished?

In addition to project evaluation, reexamine and discuss your discipling goals. Was your disciple thorough? Prompt? Organized? Creative? Did he delegate well? Was he sensitive and building to others? Did he take initiative? What did he learn?

Finally, encourage and compliment your disciple. Then when another, more difficult task arises, give him the supreme compliment—assign it to him.

Discipler's Checklist—*The Dynamics of Discipleship*
I ensure that my disciple's spiritual environment includes:
☐ Worship—an attitude of adoration that expresses our love, awe and respect for Almighty God.
☐ Ministry—building up and edifying each other.
☐ Memorization—hiding God's Word in our hearts.
☐ Meditation—striving toward God-consciousness.
☐ Teaching—
   ☐ the Bible.
   ☐ how to think.
   ☐ how to make decisions.
☐ Correcting weaknesses.
☐ Developing strengths.

12
The Disciple's Standard: Excellence

Christ's teachings have been variously interpreted as everything from idealistic ethics to legalistic commands. But no matter how others understand His teaching, a study of our Lord's life clearly reveals that He expected His disciples to *practice* what He taught them.

Jesus demanded excellence in all that His disciples did. His primary emphasis in the Sermon on the Mount, as with all His instruction, was on righteousness—the inner character which underlies outward conduct. He taught His disciples to be "perfect, as your heavenly Father is perfect" (Matthew 5:48). In the parable of the sower Jesus revealed His desire that fruit be brought to perfection (Luke 8:4–15). The crowd's evaluation of His life and ministry confirmed Christ's own commitment to excellence: ". . . He has done all things well . . ." (Mark 7:37).

God is excellent and everything He does is excellent (Psalms 119:68). Your disciple needs to understand that as a child of God his entire being must reflect the excellence of his Father. God requires him to be "perfect in every good work . . ." (Hebrews 13:21 KJV).

A person may become discouraged if he believes this expected level of performance far outweighs his capabilities.

Yet God's gifts of grace and power accompany His demands. Because Christ is in you (Colossians 1:27), righteousness is attainable.

One cold morning I took a cup of hot coffee along on my
drive to the office. I had successfully maneuvered my way
onto the freeway without spilling a drop. Suddenly, the
driver in front of me slammed on the brakes. I swerved to
avoid an accident. The coffee scalded my hand and redec-
orated the interior of my car.

Why did coffee come out of the cup? Because the man in
front of me forced me to jerk my hand? No! Coffee spilled
out of the cup because coffee was *in* the cup. Whatever was
in that cup would have come out when it was shaken.

The same is true with our behavior. When we are shaken,
the real person comes out. If another motorist takes your
parking place and your reaction is to swear, would you rationalize, "If that driver had not taken my spot, I wouldn't
have sworn"? The disciple knows that if hostility and vile
language had not been inside, the words would not have
come out.

If a scantily clad girl walks by and you lust, would you
say, "If she had not been there, I wouldn't have lusted"? A
disciple knows that if there had been no lust inside he
would not have lusted. If Christ is in you when you are
shaken, righteousness will emerge (Romans 8:10).

Discipleship is reproducing in another your experience of
Christ's involvement in your life. In order to faithfully impart a godly character to others, your disciple must understand and strive for God's standard of excellence.

Paul pinpointed for Timothy the five areas that reveal
whether a disciple is accurately reflecting his God and Father. Paul wrote, "Let no one look down on your youthful-
ness, but rather in speech, conduct, love, faith and purity,
show yourself an example of those who believe" (1 Timothy
4:12).

Speech

Your disciple's speech is an accurate barometer of his spiritual health because it reflects his character. "If any one thinks himself to be religious, and yet does not bridle his tongue but deceives his own heart, this man's religion is worthless" (James 1:26).

One morning I was talking with a pastor in the privacy of his office. To my amazement he told a dirty joke, complete with foul language. Without a moment's thought, my respect for this man plummeted. Instinctively I knew that his words reflected his heart, and this man was struggling with impurity and immaturity. Luke 6:45 teaches that ". . . his mouth speaks from that which fills his heart." A pure heart produces correct thoughts which enable us to speak in a manner pleasing to God.

God expects your disciple to control his tongue. ". . . If any one does not stumble in what he says, he is a perfect [or mature] man, able to bridle the whole body as well" (James 3:2).

James uses horseback riding to illustrate that if one fails to govern a small, seemingly insignificant part, he forfeits control over the whole. A skilled horseman knows exactly how and when to rein his horse by applying pressure on the bit. But a rider who drops the reins is helplessly out of control.

A Christian without control of his tongue is in serious danger: the tongue "corrupts the whole person, sets the whole course of his life on fire, and is itself set on fire by hell" (James 3:6 NIV). An unrestrained tongue expresses pride through boasting; it incites moral evil through off-color stories, negative humor, or racial slurs; it hypocritically blesses God even while it curses man, God's creation. Psalms 34:13 counsels, "Keep your tongue from evil, And your lips from speaking deceit."

But James 3:8 warns that no *man* can control his tongue.

However, the Holy Spirit can tame your disciple's tongue so that every word he speaks honors God and builds others. Romans 14:19 encourages us to "pursue the things which make for . . . the building up of one another."

Honesty is not always edifying. The truth can be terribly destructive. Your disciple will need to rely heavily on the Spirit's guidance in order to consistently build others without compromising the truth. He will need to correct others without undermining their will to learn. He will be called upon to stimulate excellence without thwarting the motivation to try. He will be expected to sympathetically bear others' burdens without fostering self-pity. The effectiveness of his investment in others will be largely determined by his ability to speak the truth in love. ". . . Love edifies" (1 Corinthians 8:1).

You and your disciple must pray: "Let the words of my mouth and the meditation of my heart Be acceptable in Thy sight, O Lord, my rock and my redeemer" (Psalms 19:14).

Conduct

Your disciple's behavior must produce respect for the Christ who is in him. He is exhorted to "abstain from fleshly lusts" and to keep his "behavior excellent" (1 Peter 2:11,12). His loving concern and sensitivity for others will draw people to Christ (1 Corinthians 9:19–23). This can only happen as he puts "on the new self, which in the likeness of God has been created in righteousness and holiness . . ." (Ephesians 4:24).

In order to develop excellence in your disciple, you must help him to live by his priorities. He must say no to seemingly good things that do not fit into his purpose and objectives, that do not aid his goal of making disciples. Satan often uses an abundance of opportunities as a ploy, knowing that if your disciple attempts too many things, mediocrity will characterize them all. Keeping his eye on the target will allow him to concentrate on doing everything well.

Second only to his relationship with God is his obligation to his family. One dear friend of mine was continually embarrassed by his teenage daughter. She went out of her way to do the exact opposite of everything he taught. One day he confided that her behavior was a direct result of his neglect. While he was ministering to the urgent needs of his neighbors and friends, he had ignored this foremost responsibility. Paul insists of a disciple: "He must manage his own family well and see that his children obey him with proper respect. (If anyone does not know how to manage his own family, how can he take care of God's church?)" (1 Timothy 3:4,5 NIV). Your disciple's excellence in conduct must begin at home.

Your disciple must also serve the Church with excellence. For example, it is not enough for your disciple to merely lead a Bible study. He must be well prepared and do it excellently.

When our men's staff took their teen clubs on an Easter retreat, they spent over an hour building a full-size cross out of rough timber in order to illustrate the agony of the crucifixion. They could have opted to paint a word picture instead of transporting that awkward cross all the way to the camp. But they knew that the gospel deserves an excellent presentation. And the positive response of the teens clearly verified God's blessing on their effort.

Paul instructed Titus to strive for the quality of conduct God demands: "In everything set ... an example by doing what is good. In your teaching show integrity, seriousness and soundness of speech that cannot be condemned, so that those who oppose you may be ashamed because they have nothing bad to say about us" (Titus 2:7,8 NIV).

Finally, your disciple's conduct in the world must accurately reflect his Lord. "Whatever you do, do your work heartily, as for the Lord rather than for men" (Colossians

3:23). If your disciple's behavior is patterned after Christ's, he is salt (Matthew 5:13). And a "salty Christian" causes men to thirst after God. However, if the salt becomes tasteless, it is good for nothing.

I know a Jewish accountant who is very skeptical about Christians. One day he shared with me that his prejudice against believers was rooted in one Christian's unethical financial dealings with the government. Apparently, a leader in a local church had tried to enlist my Jewish friend's assistance in defrauding the Internal Revenue Service. Even though that incident had occurred ten years earlier, the accountant had never forgotten it. Your disciple "must have a good reputation with those outside the church, so that he may not fall into reproach and the snare of the devil" (1 Timothy 3:7).

Love

Love is the sum total of Christ's law (Mark 12:30,31). Christ's perfect love for God overflowed in unconditional love for men. Matthew 8:2–4 records the story of a leper coming to Jesus to be healed. The Lord felt deep compassion for this man who had been denied human touch or physical love for most of his life. Jesus knew that his family and neighbors had fled from him, fearing that they too might contract the disease. Jesus could have cleansed this man by standing fifty feet away and simply saying the word. But the leper needed much more than physical restoration; he needed emotional healing. Moved by compassion, Jesus *touched* the leper. Imagine the exhilaration that must have shot through him—to be touched, to be loved!

Having been touched by the Son of God, the incarnation of perfect love, your disciple is both enabled and compelled to extend his hands into a world of need. His fond affection and compassion for others should make him eager to impart Christ to them (Romans 11:14).

In the inner city we have unlimited opportunities to share our love. Some of our staff have held children who were infested with lice. No one else would love or care for them. We washed them—and sometimes we got lice. Some have cleaned up alcoholics covered with their own vomit. Others have washed children whose upbringing never included personal hygiene or toilet training. We love the forgotten and neglected in order to bring glory to God. Luke 9:48 (LB) says, ". . . Your care for others is the measure of your greatness."

Faith

Your disciple must be a person of faith for without faith it is impossible to please God (Hebrews 11:6). Faith is based on facts, acting upon something that you know to be true. This contrasts with hope, which expects something to happen. Faith believes that God will or has already done it, not that He may do it. Faith is taking God at His Word.

Christ commissioned His men to make disciples of all nations, to preach the gospel to all creation (Mark 16:15). They could have spent the rest of their lives debating the improbability of accomplishing their task. How could they get to all the world? They had no airplanes or trains—not even a car. How could they reach the masses with no television, no radio, no printed plan of salvation? They didn't even have the New Testament.

But Christ had promised them authority, the power of the Holy Spirit and His continual presence. They believed Him and acted in faith upon His Word. The result is history. Their faith was proclaimed throughout the whole world (Romans 1:8) and the gospel was constantly "producing fruit and growing . . ." (Colossians 1:6 NIV).

Norm Boswell exhibited faith when he moved his wife and four young children into the ghetto of Newark to make disciples. They left Kansas before we even had a home for them. Norm had no higher education, no experience in the ghetto. People thought he was acting unreasonably. But Norm knew one thing: God had called him to preach the gospel to the poor. And the Lord promises to bless His faithful children far beyond their greatest expectations. Today, hundreds of new believers in Newark are regularly studying the Bible, disciples are being made and glory is being brought to God because of one disciple's faith.

"So faith comes from hearing, and hearing by the word of Christ" (Romans 10:17). As we study and apply God's Word, we discover that faith works! Here is the most important part of your disciple's armor (Ephesians 6:16), "for we walk by faith, not by sight" (2 Corinthians 5:7).

Without faith your disciple will have a hard time believing that Christ will use him to make disciples. Without faith God's ways appear to be foolish (1 Corinthians 2:14). But with faith ". . . everything you ask in prayer, believing, you shall receive" (Matthew 21:22).

Faith is crucial to a life of excellence because it alone enables your disciple to walk in confidence and maturity. It stands in complete opposition to a life controlled by emotions. Faith looks past circumstances to the unchanging God.

Purity

Your disciple's usefulness to God is utterly contingent upon his commitment to purity. ". . . if a man cleanses himself from these things, he will be a vessel for honor, sanctified, useful to the Master, prepared for every good work" (2 Timothy 2:21). Since God is pure He insists that His children be pure: ". . . like the Holy One who called you, be holy yourselves also in all your behavior; because it is written, 'You shall be holy, for I am holy'" (1 Peter 1:15,16). Holiness is synonymous with purity.

Purity is separation from the pollution and sin of this

world by the cleansing power of Christ's blood. God hates sin and cannot relate to impure beings without compromising His character. Everything God does is in absolute harmony with His holiness (Psalms 145:17).

First Corinthians 6:18 explains why purity is so crucial: "Flee immorality. Every other sin that a man commits is outside the body, but the immoral man sins against his own body." Sexual sin affects everything about your disciple. It colors the way he thinks of himself, resulting in insecurity and immaturity. It negatively affects his relationships with his family and other believers, making him suspicious and critical. It paralyzes his ministry by diminishing his confidence in Christ, dulling his motivation for doing God's will and robbing him of God's power. I know of no other sin which the devil has so successfully used to destroy ministries.

Since your disciple's effectiveness and the freedom of the Holy Spirit to empower him are directly affected by his holiness, you must be certain that he is pure. Unfortunately, many of us are so "saintly" that we don't even want to know if our disciple is battling for his spiritual life because of impurity. But let me be frank. If you don't love your disciple enough to ask him if he is struggling with lust, you have a shallow relationship.

Acknowledging impurity is painful. It is humbling to confess a need for continued accountability because of an ongoing battle. Nothing calls for a greater baring of one's soul. It is improbable that your disciple will admit such a problem unless he is confident that you will be compassionate and understanding and will continue to accept him.

It is too easy to respond to impurity with horror, embarrassment and condemnation. However, such an attitude could fatally wound your relationship. You must answer your disciple's cry for help by spending whatever energy is needed to pray, encourage and hold him accountable. The

Bible speaks of three elements that build your disciple's will to be pure and give him the power to walk in purity.

First, he needs to conform his mind to God's. Philippians 2:5 says, "Let this mind be in you, which was also in Christ Jesus" (KJV). Paul teaches us, ". . . whatever is true, whatever is honorable, whatever is right, whatever is pure, whatever is lovely, whatever is of good repute, if there is any excellence and if anything worthy of praise, let your mind dwell on these things" (Philippians 4:8). Your disciple's mind is of prime importance in his struggle for purity because his thoughts largely determine his behavior.

When we installed our computer, I became familiar with the acronym *GIGO. GIGO* means "garbage in—garbage out." Whatever we put into the computer determines what the computer will print out. It is only capable of using what it has been fed.

This is similar to how our minds function. If we saturate our minds with "garbage," our actions will reflect this. But if we fill our minds with God's Word, clean thoughts will then direct our mouths, hands and feet in words and acts of purity. "Every word of God is pure . . ." (Proverbs 30:5 KJV).

Second, he must be a part of a healthy, functioning Christian body. This is crucial since no disciple can maintain purity on his own. He needs the *example* of mature believers in the body, and the *protection, care* and *accountability* that only the body can provide.

Third, he must willingly confess his impurity and accept God's forgiveness. God promises that if we confess our sins, agreeing with Him about our disobedience, He will forgive us and cleanse us on the basis of His faithfulness and righteousness (1 John 1:9). Purity is impossible without receiving God's cleansing and forgiveness through confession.

However, 1 John 1:9 is not license to continue in sin. On the contrary, Proverbs 28:13 explains, ". . . he who confesses *and forsakes* [his sin] will find compassion" (*italics added*).

Your disciple's confession must be stimulated by a sincere attitude of repentance. This will be evidenced by his commitment to do everything in his power to avoid impurity.

One cold night an Arab tied up his camel beside his tent. Near midnight the old man felt the tent moving and awoke to discover his camel's nose under the flaps. When the Arab took a stick and firmly knocked the animal's nose, the camel retreated. But a little later, the camel nosed into the tent again and reasoned with the Arab: "It's so cold out here and you've got this large, warm tent. It won't hurt if I just keep my nose under the flap, will it?" After a moment's thought the Arab agreed.

About an hour later, the Arab woke up and found the camel's entire head in the tent. Quickly the animal explained, "I took just a little more room and now my head is so comfortable. It won't hurt, will it?" Once again the Arab agreed. Three more times the Arab awoke to find more of the camel's body inside the tent, and three more times he gave in to the camel's convincing pleas. Finally, the Arab awoke to find himself outside the tent and the camel sleeping snuggly inside—refusing to budge.

The moral of this story is obvious: at the first sign of impurity sneaking into your life, you must perform the venerable ritual of nose knocking. Otherwise, you will find yourself completely captivated by immorality and unable to control it.

Your disciple must strive to attain God's standard of excellence in his speech, conduct, love, faith and purity. While this ideal can be perfectly experienced only in Christ's future kingdom, God's grace and power enable us to realize a new measure of righteousness now.

Discipler's Checklist—*The Disciple's Standard: Excellence*
My disciple understands and is striving for excellence
in his:
☐ Speech
☐ Conduct
☐ Love
☐ Faith
☐ Purity

13
The Master's Model

One of my initial ventures into the business world was as a paperboy. The newspaper frequently sponsored contests to increase its circulation. I distinctly remember one pep talk from my manager: "I don't care how you get new subscriptions, just get them." The world has little concern with how the job gets done, as long as it is accomplished. How different it is in God's economy!

In discipleship the method *is* the message. Every week thousands of ghetto children attend our Bible clubs across America. We discovered that the children learn more by watching their Bible teachers love and care for others than they do by listening to the Bible story.

That's why Christ's method of training people is of the utmost importance. Careful observation of His strategy reveals that training a person to become a functioning disciple demands a two-fold approach. First, Christ's method and message was "Be like Me." Then He provided practical training over a long period of time. If either of these is missing, discipleship will not occur.

"Be Like Me"

It never ceases to amaze me how my boys try to mimic everything I do. They watch me shave and they want to shave too. They watch me jog, and they want to run up the street with me. I believe their favorite questions always begin with the same six words, "When I get bigger can I— drive your car? go to the office? use that big and noisy saw?" The intent is always the same: "When I get bigger can I—be like you?"

When Joshua and Paul were three years old they watched a neighbor and me cut down a fifty-foot eucalyptus tree in our backyard. First we trimmed off all of the lower branches to prevent damage to a nearby building. Then we felled the tree with a chain saw. The boys were absolutely delighted when the eucalyptus crashed to the ground.

The next morning I left for a trip. When I returned home, I noticed our once-full umbrella tree had been stripped of all its branches on one side. The boys were in the process of systematically pulling off every limb in preparation to saw it down.

Most of who we are today is a result of watching and listening to others. We learned how to talk by imitating our parents and other children in school. We formed personal preferences about dress, recreation, music and entertainment by copying the likes and dislikes of our family and peers. Even our thinking and philosophy of life were greatly influenced by those around us.

Making a disciple is a process that begins with being a model. Character is caught, not taught. That's why Christ's disciples left their occupations to be with Him (Mark 3:14). First, they had to follow Jesus. Only then could He train them to be "fishers of men."

The disciples accompanied Christ when He turned the water into wine. They watched Him drive the money changers out of the temple. They listened to Him minister to the Samaritan woman—in violation of a racial taboo. They saw Christ heal the nobleman's son and the lame man at Bethesda. They marveled when He cast demons out of a man at Gerasa. For months they watched Him heal the blind, the lame and the deaf. They saw Him minister to children, women, men and even His enemies. They heard extraordinary discourses, remarkable parables and the most notable message ever delivered—the Sermon on the Mount.

Jesus carefully explained His teachings and actions to His disciples so that they could understand the reasoning and principles that motivated Him. He spent time alone with them, revealing why He spoke in parables (Matthew 13:10–15) and disclosing the secrets of God's kingdom (Mark 4:11). Mark 4:34 says He explained "everything privately to His own disciples." While Jesus taught His disciples principles to follow in their ministry, He concentrated on molding their characters rather than simply imparting information. No other men have sat at the feet of a more profound, yet relevant, teacher.

What the disciples saw and heard radically affected them. They never forgot His perfect integration of teaching and doing (Acts 1:1). Faithfully they characterized Jesus as One who "went about doing good, and healing all that were oppressed . . ." (Acts 10:38). They grounded their authority in and sought credence for their message in the words, "That which we have seen and heard declare we unto you . . ." (1 John 1:3 KJV). By watching and listening to Christ, these uneducated disciples were transformed into functioning ministers, men "full of God's grace and power . . ." (Acts 6:8 NIV). Had they copied a lesser model, their ministries would have been far less significant. Antagonists later attributed the disciples' success to the fact that "they had been with Jesus" (Acts 4:13 KJV).

Jesus provided His disciples with a perfect model (John 13:15). They could then make disciples, not merely because they knew Christ, but because they had become like Him. They could model what others should become.

Like Christ, your most important task is to provide an

excellent model for your disciple. It is a law of nature that we reproduce after our own kind. We reap what we sow (Galatians 6:7,8). A farmer who plants potatoes does not expect to harvest cucumbers. Jesus said, ". . . men do not gather figs from thorns, nor do they pick grapes from a briar bush" (Luke 6:44).

This same principle is true spiritually. Only a disciple (dead to himself) can make disciples (reproduce). Note that Christ's commission to make disciples was spoken to His disciples. This is why our character must be Christ-like before we reproduce ourselves in others. We reproduce in kind for good or evil. If a carnal Christian trains another person, carnality will be the fruit of their relationship. Luke 6:40 says, "A pupil is not above his teacher; but everyone, after he has been fully trained, will be like his teacher."

When I started this ministry, I was very hesitant to confront unprepared volunteers about their lack of excellence. I'd always let it slip, hoping that God's Spirit would convict them. I even went out of my way to thank them for their effort in bothering to show up at all.

Before long I noticed this same reluctance in Al Ewert. The same fear that I had of offending and maybe losing a volunteer was reproduced in Al. I was convicted; I knew Al would never change unless he saw me change. As I grew in exercising honest confrontation based on God's standard of excellence, so did Al. While only God can produce the character of a true disciple, it is much easier for your disciple to become something he can see than something he merely hears or reads about.

I had a friend in college who aspired to be a receiver in professional football. One afternoon I was at the practice field watching him catch passes. Time after time he made spectacular receptions. The tragedy was that there were no pro scouts there watching. His ability had to be observed to be appreciated.

Your character may be impeccable, but it does your disciple little good if he is not with you to see it modeled. Paul took Timothy with him and used their experiences to flesh out biblical truths (2 Timothy 3:10,11). Let your disciple observe your life, your ministry and your love for God and others. Relax together. The more time you spend together the more effective your discipling will be. "Iron sharpens iron, So one man sharpens another" (Proverbs 27:17).

Doing things with your disciple is one of the most effective methods of modeling. You must be actively concerned about his job, finances, family relations and whatever else affects him. Teach him that as a new creation in Christ, everything he does is spiritual. If he is lax in time management, schedule his week with him. If he is weak in servanthood, do a volunteer project together. If he lacks physical discipline, jog with him every morning. If he needs to learn how to work diligently, assign a responsibility to him that requires determined effort on both of your parts. God will use your life to illustrate the practical applications of His Word.

Paul offered himself as a pattern over which his disciples could confidently trace their lives: "The things you have learned and received and heard and seen in me, practice these things; and the God of peace shall be with you" (Philippians 4:9). Paul had no fear of investing his life in his disciples. He was not ashamed to influence them because Paul did not preach about himself. He declared, "Be imitators of me, just as I also am of Christ" (1 Corinthians 11:1).

Because your character resembles the Master's, you are worth imitating. The Spirit urges and enables disciples to imitate the Christ who lives in you.

Practical Training

The first time our boys saw Katie and me swimming they wanted to jump right into the water and try it with us. Of course we could not allow two-year-olds to try swimming without proper training. First we took them in with us, holding them every moment. Then as we explained how we held our breath, shut our mouths underwater, kicked our feet and reached and pulled with our hands, they began to swim short distances on their own—as long as we were right beside them. Now they can swim the entire length of the pool by themselves. But we still watch them carefully. Someday they will be skilled enough to swim unattended.

There is no real training without involvement. Skills are developed by practically applying knowledge. Jesus was the world's greatest teacher because He perfectly balanced His disciples' theological input with their practical participation. He counseled, ". . . Be sure to put into practice what you hear. The more you do this, the more you will understand what I tell you" (Mark 4:24 LB).

Practical training necessitates involving your disciple in your life and ministry. This is accomplished through delegation. Delegating is entrusting *responsibility* and *authority* to others and establishing *accountability* for the results. These three components work together like a three-legged stool. Each is so crucial to successful delegation that if one is missing, the process topples.

Jesus was a master at training by delegation. Let's examine how He involved His disciples as He trained them in the skill of ministry.

Jesus delegated responsibility. After the disciples closely observed Christ's life and ministry and were taught the principles behind His actions, He gave them opportunities to practice what they had learned.

Their participation started with menial tasks like procuring food, distributing the loaves and fishes and securing a boat. As their commitment grew, He instructed them to baptize others. Then He took them on a trial run—a closely supervised missionary journey through Galilee. They became His associates in ministry.

Soon Jesus gave them assignments to carry out with only
limited supervision (Matthew 10:7,8). He commissioned
them to preach the gospel and heal the sick. In order to help
them accomplish this task, He gave them guidelines within
which they could decide how to act in various situations:
what to preach, how to minister to men in need, where to
go, what to take along, how to finance their trip and how to
respond to opposition. Jesus designed the disciples' educational experience not only to meet the spiritual and physical
needs of their neighbors but also to build their confidence
and maturity.

Four guidelines will help you effectively delegate responsibility to your disciple:

1. *Never delegate prematurely.* Premature delegation
   feeds pride and reinforces the world's thinking that
   abilities and talents produce fruit. It infers that
   "doing" is more important than "being" and reflects
   the mentality that ministering and discipling are
   man's work instead of the work of the Spirit. Delegate responsibility on the basis of your disciple's
   self-death, servanthood and maturity, not skills.

   Do not assume that your disciple knows how to
   carry out the responsibility you are assigning to him
   unless you have done it with him or have seen him do
   it. A good teacher trains his student by example.
   Your disciple learns how to minister by watching you
   minister and by ministering with you. Be sure he is
   capable and knows how to perform the responsibility
   you delegate to him.
2. *Delegate clearly.* Specifically define the responsibility
   your disciple is to assume. Be sure he thoroughly understands the results you expect.

3. *Delegate gradually.* Initially you will do everything together. Delegating responsibility begins slowly. Start by assigning small tasks which have a high probability of success. Failure creates insecurity. Help him avoid unnecessary mistakes which would damage his confidence. As he gains experience and matures spiritually, give him larger jobs. Luke 16:10 says, "He who is faithful in a very little thing is faithful also in much; and he who is unrighteous in a very little thing is unrighteous also in much."

While there are certain responsibilities and decisions that you cannot relinquish, you should delegate as much as possible. The men that Christ trained delegated responsibility liberally (1 Peter 5:1–4; Titus 3:8).

4. *Inspire confidence.* Your disciple must know that you are confident in his ability to accomplish the assigned task. Tell him about the growth you observe in his life. Paul delighted in the growth of those whom he served: ". . . your faith is greatly enlarged, and the love of each one of you toward one another grows ever greater; therefore, we ourselves speak proudly of you . . ." (2 Thessalonians 1:3, 4). He applauded Philemon for his love and faith (Philemon 4, 5). Encourage and praise your disciple for jobs well-done.

Offer constructive criticism which leads to improvement rather than dwelling on temporary failures. Your attitude, more than your words, will build confidence. Be sure he feels he is making a significant contribution and has a vital ministry. Demonstrate your confidence by asking his opinion on specific problems and follow his advice when possible.

Jesus delegated authority. Christ gave His disciples the *authority* to accomplish their responsibilities of healing the sick and proclaiming the kingdom. "... He gave them authority over unclean spirits, to cast them out, and to heal every kind of disease and every kind of sickness" (Matthew 10:1).

Responsibility and authority must be equally delegated. It is unfair to ask your disciple to accept a responsibility for which you are unwilling to give sufficient authority. Insufficient authority leads to frustration and inefficiency. Why assign a task if your disciple must continually consult you in order to secure the authority to make decisions? Once you entrust a responsibility to him, let him lead.

Based on your past experience and the input of your leaders, decide how much authority will be required to carry out the responsibility you have assigned to your disciple. Then specifically define the extent of this authority. Be sure your disciple understands these limits. For example, you can set financial boundaries. If you assign the task of taking forty-five children on a field trip, you can specify that he should spend no more than $100. While he has the freedom to decide how to transport the children and what to feed them, he knows that his gas and food expenses cannot exceed $100 unless he receives your additional authorization.

Along with the delegation of responsibility and authority comes the "right" to be wrong. Your disciple will make mistakes and wrong decisions. We all do. Find out where he went wrong. Then help him to see where his thinking broke down. Encouraging your disciple to use failures as stepping-stones to future growth will help him focus on improving his ministry, not on defending himself.

Jesus exercised accountability. Christ loved His disciples so much that He evaluated and corrected their actions so that they could grow in their Christian walk. He held them accountable. After the disciples' first "solo" missionary journey, they "gathered together with Jesus; and they reported to Him all that they had done and taught" (Mark 6:30). No doubt Jesus evaluated their work and reviewed the goals He had assigned to them. This time of sharing refined their ministry skills.

The tragedy in the Church today is that so few people are willing to make the necessary time and emotional invest-ment in .another that accountability requires. Before your discipling relationship began you promised to promote growth by holding your disciple accountable. Do not fail him.

Provide accountability and personal guidance in every as-pect of your disciple's life and ministry. Encourage him in regular Bible study, Scripture memorization, meditation, prayer and worship. When his behavior and attitudes are not excellent, you must help him correct his weaknesses and develop his strengths.

Withdrawal

When Jesus was confident that His men had been trained, He handed over to them the leadership of God's work on earth and commissioned them to make disciples every-where. *Before* Christ was crucified, He prayed to the Father, "I have brought you glory on earth by completing the work you gave me to do" (John 17:4 NIV). Christ's work was to train men, not simply to perform miracles or preach the gospel. When He had equipped His disciples, He could confidently ask to rejoin the Father (John 17:5).

Withdrawal is the final step in training your disciple how to minister. Withdrawal begins when your disciple is equipped to start discipling others. You repeat the same process you went through of praying for and carefully choosing a disciple in whom to invest. However, this time both you and your disciple are equipped for reproduction. Consequently, you are praying for two additional people.

When your disciple begins to disciple another person,

your relationship continues, but the focus changes, even as Christ's relationship with His disciples changed after His ascension. Now you concentrate on helping him to train another person to become a functioning disciple.

The Master's method was "Be like Me," coupled with practical training that led to His withdrawal. We are wise to follow His example.

I am convinced that training others to train others is one of the greatest joys Christ allows us to experience. But it demands an enormous concentration of energy and will. My challenge to you is to BE God's person, rest in His sovereignty and let Him work freely through you in this most exciting part of building His kingdom.

Discipler's Checklist—*The Master's Model*
☐ I provide an excellent model for my disciple.
☐ I provide practical training.
  ☐ I delegate responsibility.
  ☐ I delegate authority.
  ☐ I exercise accountability.

Keith Phillips is president of World Impact, a Christian missions organization dedicated to bringing God's love to the ghettos of America. His first book, *They Dare to Love the Ghetto*, graphically describes this modern-day missionary thrust. You can acquire this 192-page book by sending $2.00 to World Impact at the address below.

For information on how you can become involved in World Impact's vital discipleship ministry through prayer, financial support or as a full-time staff member, write or call:

WORLD IMPACT, INC.
2001 So. Vermont Ave.
Los Angeles, CA 90007
(213) 735-1137